Designing Architecture

Designing Architecture is an indispensible tool to assist both students and young architects in formulating an idea, transforming it into a building, and making effective design decisions. This book promotes integrative and critical thinking in the preliminary design of buildings to inspire creativity, innovation, and design excellence.

This compendium of individual wisdom and collective experience offers explicit guidance on how to approach, analyze, and execute specific tasks; develop and refine a process to facilitate the best possible design projects; and create meaningful architectural form. Here the design process—from orchestrating client participation to finalizing schematic design—is explored and illuminated. The book presents:

- explicit strategies for doing design rather than simply reviewing principles and precedents
- creative ideas in approaching and framing problems in design terms
- specific methods to translate ideas into culturally significant, socially responsive, and environmentally sensitive buildings
- techniques to integrate all levels of cognition from analysis to epiphany
- counsel on developing a personalized process for engaging design projects
- case studies augmenting the text and chronicling fascinating applications of the design process.

The essence of this book lies in an integrated and holistic approach to each unique project as well as fostering curiosity and exploration—a departure from algorithms, easy generalities, or a formula for design. *Designing Architecture* will inspire readers to elevate the quality of preliminary designs and unravel some of the mystery of creating the most beautiful, responsive, and responsible architectural design possible.

Andrew Pressman, FAIA, an architect and Professor Emeritus at the University of New Mexico, leads his own architectural firm in Washington, D.C. His work has been featured in over 30 professional, scholarly, and popular publications. He has written six critically acclaimed books and holds a Master's degree from the Harvard University Graduate School of Design.

To Lisa, my sweetheart; and to Samantha and Daniel, who are constant reminders to view the world as all architects should: With fresh and positive perspective, intelligence, humor, confidence, and above all, playfulness, joy, and wonder.

Andrew Pressman

First published 2012
by Routledge
2 Park Square, Milton Park, Abingdon, Oxon OX14 4RN

Simultaneously published in the USA and Canada
by Routledge
711 Third Avenue, New York, NY 10017

Routledge is an imprint of the Taylor & Francis Group, an informa business

British Library Cataloguing in Publication Data
A catalogue record for this book is available from the British Library

Library of Congress Cataloging in Publication Data
Pressman, Andy.
Designing architecture : the elements of process / Andrew Pressman.
p. cm.
Includes index.
1. Architectural design. I. Title. II. Title: Elements of process.
NA2750.P6953 2012
720--dc22
2011016356

ISBN: 978-0-415-59515-5 (hbk)
ISBN: 978-0-415-59516-2 (pbk)
ISBN: 978-0-203-12217-4 (ebk)

Typeset in Caslon by Gavin Ambrose
Printed and bound in Great Britain by Bell & Bain Ltd., Glasgow

Designing Architecture
The elements of process

Andrew Pressman

 Routledge
Taylor & Francis Group

LONDON AND NEW YORK

Contents

1

Introduction to the design process   15

2

Influences and inspiration   33

3

Doing design   95

4

Case studies   159

Foreword

Doing architecture is hard. But teaching architecture is even harder. Andrew Pressman makes the teaching of architecture appear effortless, as he takes us on a great journey in learning (or re-learning) the most important aspects of architectural design. This book is for the budding architect still in school and for the blossoming architect now in practice. Pressman also has many wise things to tell architects who have been at it for years and may have gotten lost along the way. If you have reached the point in your architecture career where you find yourself slumped at a desk, staring out of a window, and wondering where the magic went, read this book.

We architects spend many of our waking moments immersed in and, at night, dreaming about the culture of our art, science, and theory. Central to Pressman's message is that architecture has an important purpose outside this insular world of architecture. This book reminds us that, above everything else, we have a responsibility to the client and to the people who will live, work, and play in the environments we design for many years after we design them. Exploring design ideas, finding solutions to problems, creating buildings that inspire, making a statement through architecture— all these attractive, seductive possibilities propel us. But ultimately, it's not about us. It's about all the lives that our designs will touch. No pressure, right?

Design can be mysterious. The author helps us see through the mix of notions, ideas, and inspirations that we carry around with us and want to infuse into our architecture. How does design begin? It starts with a client's dream, a program, a site, the services that a building must perform. As architects we absorb all of this (and much more) inside ourselves, let it steep, and then pour it out through our drawings and models. A huge part of design is watching and listening before we begin to draw. Pressman gives us sound guidance on the many things to listen and watch for, how to analyze them, and how to apply them. He shows us techniques that can transform good information into sound design. Communication is critical. Much of an architect's work is telling the story about a building that will make others want to see it built. Consultants, colleagues, and others become part of this narrative and it becomes richer as it is told and retold. Design is iterative—

loops of information-gathering, drawing, discussing, thinking, rethinking—
until a work of architecture emerges.

Architects have many tools for visualization at their disposal, all of which are
discussed here. Finding and using the right tool to fashion a design solution
is a bit like woodworking—it takes practice. Drawing, model-making,
and digital media are not just methods to communicate an idea already
formed—they are more valuable used as tools to explore design. Working
on a drawing or a model is another form of conversation—between you and
the design, back and forth. Suddenly you see something you didn't know
was there. Turn the model around and there's an idea you didn't realize you
had. Push it further, make another drawing, build another model. What's the
lesson? There are no shortcuts, so lay in a good supply of pens and blades.

Architectural design is a challenge because there is never just one answer.
This is what makes it simultaneously thrilling and terrifying. As you move
along toward an answer, many paths (some chosen, others ignored) will
shape the building. Architectural design is a world of "divergent" solutions.
A roomful of mathematicians will work to "converge" on the right answer;
architects take a design problem and diverge in as many directions as there
are architects, each one creating his or her solution. Some solutions are
better than others. This book will guide you to getting a better answer,
without telling you what the answer should be.

*Michael J. Crosbie, Ph.D., AIA, who has written extensively about architecture and
design, is Chair of the University of Hartford Department of Architecture.*

Preface

Designing Architecture aims to provide help in formulating an idea, transforming it into a building, and making effective design decisions. The book promotes integrative and critical thinking in the preliminary design of buildings to inspire creativity, innovation, and design excellence.

Designing Architecture is intended to assist students and young professionals alike in creating excellent designs, even magical buildings, evoking the admirable vision that launches most prospective architects into the profession. This compendium of individual wisdom and collective experience offers explicit guidance on how to approach, analyze, and execute specific tasks; develop and refine a process to facilitate innovative design projects; and create meaningful architectural form.

I have endeavored to use ideologically neutral terms so that readers with diverse backgrounds, experience, and perspectives will embrace the book and benefit more fully from its use. My intention is that readers will find the material that is useful to them, wherever it appears in the book. The very practical content will speak to beginning students, while the more advanced content will reach and mean something more to the experienced reader.

Design processes, from orchestrating client participation to finalizing schematics, will be explored and illuminated. The essentially applications-oriented point of view is informed by insights from professional practice and from the halls and studios of the academy. Graphic examples of components of actual design processes from noteworthy practitioners elucidate ideas in full color, and provide windows on achieving design excellence.

The book also promotes critical reflection about the significance of architecture beyond function and budget—although those issues are considered as well. This may be one way to begin to define design excellence. As suggested throughout the book, design excellence also requires cultivating the habit of observing and documenting detail and critically monitoring creative thinking. Nothing is that special or brilliant that it cannot be modified for the good of a project.

The following material is presented to make *Designing Architecture* a useful didactic tool for both student and professional development:

- strategies for doing design rather than simply reviewing principles and precedents
- ideas in approaching and framing problems in design terms.
- methods to translate ideas to culturally significant, socially responsive, and environmentally sensitive buildings
- techniques to integrate all levels of cognition from analysis to epiphany
- counsel on developing a personalized process for engaging design projects
- advice on how to infuse projects with your particular brand of energy and remain open to evolving possibilities.

This book, therefore, does not provide a universal method or formula for designing. Its essence lies in proposing an integrated and holistic approach to each unique project as well as fostering curiosity and exploration—a departure from algorithms and easy generalities. Thus, at its most idealistic, perhaps this work will offer fuel for the creative fire and support confidence that the outcome will be nothing less than excellent.

The architectural design process is a powerful but sometimes elusive mechanism for solving problems. It is tempting to posit that most challenges in life may be reduced to a design problem and effectively managed as such. So flexible and enlightening is the refined process of design that the failure of other disciplines to adapt and apply it seems most surprising.

Pilots provide an unwitting example of the design process in a different context. One can readily imagine the scenario: It is midnight and we are making an approach on instruments to a rural airstrip, the gateway to a long-awaited winter skiing vacation. The forecast was way off; the front's arrival surprised everyone. The clouds have been dense with ice, now gradually building up on the leading edges of the wings. While a fair amount of fuel has burned off, we are still heavy with luggage, skis, two kids, two adults, and a dog. I shudder to think how much weight we're picking up with that ice. The flight controls are increasingly sluggish, and the GPS is suddenly on the fritz. I'm not sure I can trust the airspeed indicator with the ice buildup outside on the instruments. We're in the mountains, the visibility couldn't be worse, and suddenly there is an electrical failure. The artificial horizon and radio altimeter are out, the engine is straining, I don't know where we are, and I've got to set us down. I reduce power and as we descend, we lose some weight as chunks of ice slide off the wings. I pray they won't strike the tail control surfaces. Finally, I see it! The runway appears. I try to gauge the wind as I forgo a downwind leg and turn a short base. The little engine is running on vapor.

I develop a rhythm to control the descent, applying and pulling off the throttle, and making adjustments with the yoke and rudder pedals. The entire constellation of variables suddenly seems to come together, somehow the ambiguous and the contradictory become defined and make sense. The runway threshold flashes by beneath the nose as I cut what's left of the power, feather the prop, drop the rest of the flaps, and begin gently tapping the toe brakes.

Indeed, the traits that make a good aviator are those required of a successful architect. This book hopes to reveal and enable those traits. An architect relies on a great fund of knowledge as well as integrative skills to shape a solution. Again, as in aviation, the best architects also rely on feelings, intuition, and common sense. Couple this with an openness to joy and inspiration and the result is great flying and extraordinary architecture.

Designing Architecture will be of great practical value to those who have been indoctrinated to believe that architectural design is mystical or so ridden with complexity and contradiction that it really cannot be taught. As with any of the great professions, valuable continuing education in architecture must rest upon a foundation of specialized knowledge, acquisition of focused skills, systematic development of talent, and practice. *Designing Architecture* is intended to augment this foundation and serve as a creative trigger for design ideas.

At its grandest, architecture (and architects) can have enduring effects on society. At its most mundane, architecture can have an influence on the quality of a day—and, to paraphrase Thoreau, that may be the highest of arts. I trust this book has marshaled sufficient evidence to support these assertions and remind us of the really noble and creative possibilities intrinsic to the profession.

Coverage of topics strives to be accessible and comprehensive yet digestible to crystallize the essence of process. It is perilously easy to appreciate and focus on detail at the expense of the globally important. I submit that a great many of our professional errors arise from such a failure in cognition. It is therefore my fondest hope that *Designing Architecture* will enhance the vision of students and young architects to provide a lens through which the truly significant is rendered clear, and responsive and responsible architectural design is created.

Andrew Pressman, FAIA
Washington, D.C.
April 2011

Acknowledgments

Much appreciation, respect, and gratitude are extended to Francesca Ford, Commissioning Editor at Routledge, for recognizing the value of the undertaking, providing cogent suggestions, and for her professionalism throughout the process. I am grateful to the production and design team at Taylor & Francis (Kyle Duggan, Gavin Ambrose, Laura Williamson and Faith McDonald) for their truly outstanding work.

The following individuals deserve special mention for keen editorial advice and guidance: Don Hanlon, Mark C. Childs, Catharine Lisa Kauffman, Peter Pressman, and Iris Slikerman.

Special thanks to Michael J. Crosbie for writing the Foreword and to Stephen D. Dent for writing the sidebar on building performance. I am grateful to Roger Goldstein and Scott Simpson, respectively, for the Goody Clancy and KlingStubbins case studies, and Phil Bernstein and Joy Stark for the sidebar on conceptual design on the computer.

Many thanks to Tim Stephenson for helping to make this project a reality, Norm Weinstein for stimulating e-conversations, and T.J. Meehan for input on computing and design.

Appreciation is extended to the following individuals and organizations (in alphabetical order) whose graphic material dramatically enriches the content herein: Geoffrey Adams, Jason Alread, Centre Culturel Tjibaou, Katie Clark/IDEO, Michael Dickson, Mike Doherty, Ed Ford, Kirk Gittings, Tim Hursley, Jim Leggitt, Laura Lesniewski, Roger Lewis, John Linden, Jennifer Masengarb, Norman McGrath, Moore Ruble Yudell Architects & Planners, Murphy/Jahn Architects, Raymond Novitske, Steve Oles, Pei Cobb Freed & Partners Architects LLP, John Petronis, Antoine Predock, Steve Rosenthal, Christopher Spielmann, James Steeves, Lara Swimmer, and David Vaughan.

Figure credits
All designs, photographs, and drawings are by Andrew Pressman, FAIA, unless otherwise noted.

"When the character of space moves someone, outside the analytic discussion of design work, or sustainability, or the myriad other elements that can be articulated and quantified, that's architecture."

Antoine Predock[0]

Chapter 1
Introduction to the design process

"Well, well, I… to me—I… I mean, it's–it's—it's all instinctive, you know. I mean, I just try to uh, feel it, you know? I try to get a sense of it and not think about it so much".

Annie Hall (from the screenplay by Woody Allen and Marshall Brickman)[1]

Notwithstanding Annie Hall's ditzy description of her pursuit of the art of photography, reflecting on the art of architectural design can be enormously beneficial. While it may be debatable that instinct and epiphany are necessary to be a great designer, the design process, by and large—including all the ingredients necessary to achieve great design—ought to be absolutely learnable. Thinking critically about design ideas, client and stakeholder requirements, a project's unique site and context, and the resources available to complete the project are fundamental to developing preliminary designs. While there is no magic formula, these components can be studied, systematically characterized, and rationally wedded to a process that yields effective design.

Most of the distinctive variables that shape the design process are driven by the specifics of the project circumstance, i.e., the site, program, client, and so on, and therefore are, by definition, unique to each project. A fresh gestalt arises with each and every project, which is what makes architecture so fascinating and exciting! The process can be just as creative and unique as the product.

Architectural design really starts with the way in which the program or brief—the inventory of needs—is read, how the problems are defined and interpreted, how the client is engaged, and even how background research is conducted and information collected. Assessing a site, visualizing possibilities, arranging bubbles of spaces on a site plan or in one's mind, and formulating concepts are all very creative activities that comprise the first stages of design.

Design, broadly defined (see Sidebar 1.1), is an all-inclusive way of looking at and addressing problems that starts from project inception, extends into the final phases of construction, and, in some cases, for the life cycle of the building. Design is not something that is tacked on after analysis, or after solving the space-planning puzzle; nor is it purely aesthetic. The unsung element is the set of intangibles or cognitive processes that arise from a passionate and deeply personal involvement—with a project at every step of its development—from engaging clients to examining materials, components, and systems, to construction.

Antoine Predock, FAIA, says of the design process, "Projects coalesce both from rigorous research and pure intuition."[2] Indeed, this intuition, talent, or instinct informed by the program, site, and concept will likely lead to the creation of great architecture.

Process elements and iterative loops

So, how do we break down "design" into a process and components that can be defined and applied in practice? Process is about thoughts and feelings that become intertwined and assume a certain magnitude and direction. It is necessarily vague, individualized, and always evolves. It is the great "x-factor," the thing we as architects tend to prize above all else. Forced to find the objective in process, I would characterize it as iterative, requiring successive loops, each of which produces more information and resolution than the previous one. The resolution may crystallize or suggest reframing of problems and questions to be addressed. A representative loop consists of a number of steps, which are described below (see also Figure 1.1). Certainly there are variations in focus, content, and sequence of the steps as a function of designer and project idiosyncrasies, and some steps may even be skipped or combined.

Some of the more standardized cognitive aspects of the design process may be viewed as elements, as follows:

Problem definition. The program describes the design issues and usually includes functional requirements and relationships, in both qualitative and quantitative terms. Budget, schedule, and quality as well as expectations and aspirations are all discussed and documented.

Information gathering. Begin research by examining precedents (similar building types and local design and construction techniques), identifying applicable codes and regulations, and collecting an array of site and climate data including the immediate context and region.

Analysis. Rigorous analysis is a meaningful prerequisite for designing; it results in a clear, orderly, and fine-grained view of the problem, and may be a trigger for innovative design ideas. Converting program, cost, site, and other data into graphic forms (including identifying possible relationships and patterns) can be analytically illuminating.

Synthesis leading to diagrammatic schemes. Consider and combine various project influences to create concepts, develop program and site relationships, circulation patterns, environmental strategies, and aesthetic ideas including investigations of three-dimensional form possibilities.

Schematic design development. This element suggests a more resolved version of the diagrammatic schemes and includes materials selections, building systems and their integration, proposals for construction technology and detailing, building performance, and a vision of what it would be like to experience the building.

Soliciting and responding to critical feedback. Here is an opportunity to make the project better; to validate concepts and solutions (relative to the problem definition) by subjecting them to invited critical appraisal from both stakeholders and colleagues. Conversely, schemes may be so innovative and deliver outcomes never imagined that initial ideas are rendered obsolete.

A slightly different way of imagining the design process is described by Tim Brown, head of IDEO, an innovation and design firm in Palo Alto. He says: "The design process is best described metaphorically as a system of spaces rather than a predefined series of orderly steps. The spaces demarcate different sorts of related activities that together form the continuum of innovation."[3] Brown tags the three spaces as follows. (1) *Inspiration*—for the circumstances (i.e., problems, opportunities) that motivate the search for solutions; (2) *ideation*—for the process of generating, developing, and testing ideas that may lead to solutions; and (3) *implementation*—for the charting of a path to market (or in the case of architecture, developing construction documents and constructing the building). Just as with the iterative loops described above, as projects evolve, they pass through the first two "spaces" multiple times (see Figure 1.2).

While seemingly contradictory, implicit in the design process is a focus on the big picture and small detail at the same time. This parallel focus implies that work must be infused with both technical acumen and design sensitivity—even during the early stages.

Norman Rosenfeld
Good design—you know it when you see it: an Eames chair, a Brancusi sculpture, the chapel at M.I.T. Good architectural design is the perfect union of material, form, space, and light providing a special presence—an enclosure or environment appropriate to the charge.

Don Schlegel
Architecture is a concept, an idea that captures the spirit of truth, time, and place. Architectural truth respects form and function, construction, and material. Architectural time respects the epoch of its design origin. Architectural place respects the context of its culture, climate, and topology.

Antoine Predock
"What is good design?" is so elusive to answer, and even define. Just repeating it here doesn't do justice to its true meaning, and any attempt to respond will never approach its awesome promise. You can say, however, that a great building not only has qualities that move you, but has the capacity to enrich by experiencing many journeys through it: rational journeys of the intellect, choreographic journeys that are very physical, journeys that have to do with the unknown—the unexpected spatial possibilities that surprise and arrest you. Then there is the realm of light as animator that shapes and conditions these journeys. So, you may begin to inventory the elements.

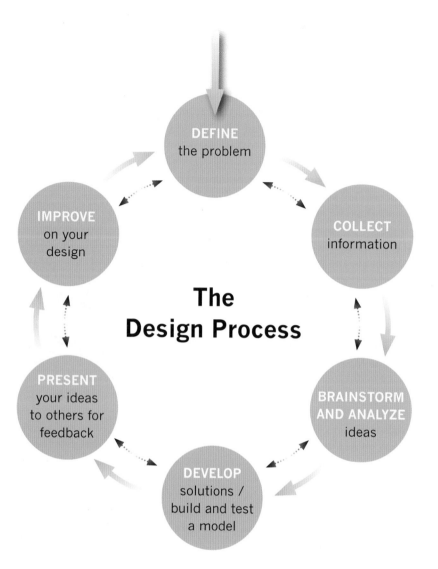

Figure 1.1
A graphic example of the various components of the design process (© Chicago Architecture Foundation, *The Architecture Handbook*).

Creativity and epiphany

Imagination, epiphany, innovation, and creativity: As traditionally elusive as these notions are that define the magical element of what we do, there is nonetheless some critical intangible that separates minimally competent practice from great design, even genius. While the intangibles almost by definition may not be teachable, they must be discussed and nurtured in each of us, whatever specific contribution they may underlie. For example, some of us recall specific precedents, a unique site feature, or perhaps a new material. Then when these images activate something in your own soul and move you to express it on paper, you build a model; then you rip it apart, change something, and rebuild. Whatever one's creative process may be, it must be illuminated, constantly refined, and consciously integrated with the more formal and disciplined components of design.

Several distinguished architects cited below address both the interpretive aspects as well as the objective methodology of design.

Increasingly, we recognize that the design process works with information and ideas simultaneously on many levels. Thus, the architect can be thinking simultaneously about the overall geometry of the building, the ways in which a wheelchair-bound person might experience the spaces in the building, and the materials of which the building will be constructed.

Bradford Perkins, FAIA[4]

As always, the process consists of questions built upon questions: What if? If this goes here, will this fit there? What is the appropriate hierarchy between this sequence of rooms? What are the sight lines and sources of light inside the house? What are the views from inside to outside— and from outside to inside? If I arrange the bedrooms at opposite ends of the house instead of above or below, how would that alter the client's expectations of interior zoning? Are there ways to profitably impose or disrupt a rhythm of elements (windows, doors, posts, beams, corners, casework, stairs), expand a space, or condense it down? Can I gain a sense of openness by letting a wall stop short of a ceiling—and still retain a sense of privacy? Some ideas begin to suggest others, some lead nowhere. As I prove and disprove each thesis, the search will lead to something that may work. Or not.

Don Metz[5]

When I work on the programming phase of a building, I'm in there. It isn't just about square footages and relationships and bubble diagrams, it's about intangibles paralleling those kinds of things. I insist that my clients fantasize and dream in the programming phase, just as much as when the evolutionary process of making a building is happening.

Antoine Predock, FAIA[6]

We are very question/answer oriented. Ours is a classically heuristic approach in which we attend to a process to arrive at a solution rather than to begin from an a priori position. Many people think architects are solution oriented. The discussion we're having is actually about exploring a problem and articulating questions, which become the focus of our design investigations. The viability of the methodology is based on the question-posing process, which is an inclusive process designed to elicit creativity rather than to inhibit it.

Thom Mayne, FAIA[7]

What I believe the architects inventoried above have wrestled with is the effort to give voice to a multi-factorial, even chaotic process. Despite the angst, there is an overarching sense of comfort, especially with the inherent ambiguity; anything is possible. The freedom to create is exhilarating.

Design attitude

In our evolving practice environment, it behoves all of us as architects to think critically about the design process—service and project delivery—and apply as much design thinking to shape the process as to creating buildings. Constantly reflecting on and improving your own personal design process will undoubtedly result in buildings that are better functionally, technically, and aesthetically. Keep in mind that a dash of personality, of playfulness and spontaneity, serves to temper the proper but often stultifying gravity of complex projects. There is energy and perspective in humor. Comic relief can be just that, imparting much-needed relaxation and refreshment in scalable fashion. Here are some tips for engaging the process.

Become immersed in the circumstances of the project. Design clues will emerge and become evident the deeper you go and the more fully the issues are understood. "The personality of the client, the region that it's in, and the place where it is … it's a discovery process that you go through for each project, and hopefully at the outcome there's something unique for that particular exercise, that project,"[8] says Merrill Elam of Mack Scogin Merrill Elam Architects.

Collaboration and teamwork can add richness and depth to a project. Constructive and inspiring conversations—whether they are with stakeholders, engineering consultants, constructors, vendors, or other design professionals—can somehow become synergistic. "A kind of healthy instability would characterize the process of how we work. It's based on collegiality, collaboration, discourse exchange, and a fair number of arguments,"[9] says Shirley Blumberg of KPMB.

Embrace ambiguity. Even the most promising project will have many unknowns. And new information may be brought to bear after work on the project is initiated. "In the search for that 'Eureka!' moment of a great design solution, we must often follow unclear instincts, fuzzy clues, or paths that seem to hold no promise. Yet, it is through this ambiguous terrain that we come to find our best solutions,"[10] says Clark Kellogg, Kellogg Communications.

Have confidence in the design process and trust your intuition. But it may take some time and experience to reach that point. "To a large extent, beginnings are always extremely fragile and ideas easily defeated. I think design beginnings require a conviction about the end; a belief that following your path will ultimately get you to something strong,"[11] says Michael Maltzan of Michael Maltzan Architecture.

Do something different. Change the way you work to foster creativity. "Change drives my work, and it is as important to the creative process as habit is…. Fundamental change is an endeavor, it's a real enterprise, it's not something that just happens. You make a choice to keep evolving and keep growing,"[12] says choreographer Twyla Tharp.

Another perspective about design attitude is exemplified in characteristics of design thinkers, articulated by Tim Brown, head of IDEO. Those characteristics are distilled as follows:[13]

- *Empathy*. Imagine the world from multiple perspectives. This will enable noticing things that others do not, which will inspire innovation.

- *Integrative thinking*. See all of the salient—and sometimes contradictory—aspects of a confounding problem to dramatically improve existing alternatives.

- *Optimism*. Assume that no matter how challenging the constraints of a given problem, at least one potential solution is better than existing alternatives.

- *Experimentalism*. Pose questions and explore constraints in creative ways that proceed in entirely new directions.

- *Collaboration*. Replace the myth of the lone creative genius with the reality of the enthusiastic interdisciplinary collaborator.

Maintaining openness to visualizing the experience of the building at the earliest stages of design can trigger innovation and bring the project to life. One way to begin designing the experience of the project is to create a narrative vision or story of what a journey through the building might be like. Bryan Lawson suggests in *How Designers Think* that employing vocabulary in such narratives that is "evocative without being too prescriptive"[14] can spark multiple interpretations by the design team and thus lead to alternative and innovative schemes.

Imagining different scenarios—events, mixes of people, and times—will facilitate examining the problem in fresh ways and designing robust physical spaces to accommodate those scenarios. Norman Weinstein cites an example:

> The freshest new architecture in my city—Boise, Idaho—is an art gallery initially constructed through a writing exercise. The architect presented a plan to the client: Both would spend a week writing an uninhibited, extravagant, richly imaginative description of the proposed gallery. They would then meet and discuss their writing. Surprisingly, each wrote a description of an uncannily similar design originally inspired by the designs of the Japanese architect Tadao Ando. The gallery was written into existence, a mutual weave of writing as much a part of its foundation as poured concrete.[15]

Figure 1.2
The design process as conceived
by IDEO is best described
metaphorically as a system of spaces
rather than a predefined series of
orderly steps (courtesy of IDEO).

IMPLEMENTATION

INSPIRATION

1

Move onto the next
project – repeat

Expect Success
Build implementation resources into your plan

Make the case to the business
– spread the word

3

Help marketing design a
communication strategy

What's the business problem?
Where's the opportunity? What has
changed (or soon may change)?

Look at the world: observe what
people do, how they think, what
they need and want

Execute the Vision
Engineer the experience

What are the business constraints
(time, lack of resources,
impoverished customer base,
shrinking market)?

Prototype some more, test with
users, test internally

Involve many disciplines from
the start (e.g. engineering and
marketing)

Pay close attention to "extreme"
users such as children or the elderly

Communicate internally –
don't work in the dark!

Have a project room
where you can share
insights, tell stories

Tell more stories (they keep
ideas alive)

Prototype, test,
Prototype, test...

How can new technology help?

Apply integrative thinking

Put customers in the midst
of everything; describe
their journeys

Build creative frameworks
(order out of chaos)

Make many sketches,
concoct scenarios

Are valuable ideas, assets and
expertise hiding inside the business?

Brainstorm

Organize information and sythesize
possibilities (tell more stories!)

2

IDEATION

Architectural concepts

In the broadest sense, an architectural concept is a device that integrates program, site, and other factors toward the creation of a functional or symbolic theme in support of an emerging design. "Parti" is a term frequently used in jargon-laden dialogue, and is essentially interchangeable with "concept." It refers to the essential formative scheme, idea, or basic organizing principle of a building design. The cliché: "The whole is greater than the sum of its parts" is another way to describe the role of an architectural concept. This notion can be viewed as a construct that supports the assembly of disparate elements into some magical building composition.

Formulating a concept for a project at its inception is critical to developing architecture, making decisions at every step in the process, and gaining insight into the project's soul. A strong initial idea is valuable because design decisions can be imprinted by it and then relate to it (or even express it), thereby ensuring coherence among all elements of a project—from large-scale site planning to the smallest construction detail. When design decisions are less arbitrary, i.e., they are informed by the concept, the architecture becomes greater, more powerful, and meaningful. (As an extreme example, even the design of the letterhead for the building's inhabitants could reflect the architectural concept.) A bold idea can generally weather limited budgets, tight schedules, codes and regulations, and inevitable changes during the design process without diluting its power. A great idea can motivate you to jump gracefully through all the hoops and endure the marathon required to get a project built. On the other hand, if gymnastics are required to make an idea work, then it's probably not the right one, and the wise architect remains open to new possibilities.

The solitary subjective contribution to concept that we gloss over, avoid altogether, or at the other extreme, idealize, is what I would term the architect's personality or personal vision. Roots of form making that can be attributed to personal vision, that seem surprisingly independent of circumstance, and that appear across projects as a genealogy of buildings include works by Frank Gehry, Richard Meier, Thom Mayne, Michael Graves, and so on. Throughout our history, we have alternately elevated and suppressed the value of the designer's personality as manifest in the work, but it remains the proverbial 800-pound gorilla who sits at our table. Arguably, even the spare designs of the modern movement were as much the product of distinct and powerful personalities as they were functional responses to socio-cultural and other forces of the time. My point here is that the personal traits and vision of the architect are in fact salient and should be acknowledged and even embraced. This is, after all, one of the factors that differentiates us as professionals from technicians or software.

Here are several examples of strong architectural concepts.

● Anne Taylor, Ph.D., an expert in school facility programming, proposed a concept for a primary school in New Mexico: Her concept of a school as a three-dimensional textbook is a mandate to create a direct linkage of the physical environment to learning and curriculum. This demonstrates how a single phrase— "three-dimensional textbook"[16]—can be so evocative and can inspire creative thinking about integration and expression of complex building systems, assemblies, and components in meaningful ways.

Figure 1.3
This diagram is a simplified accounting of the ingredients of design. Interaction between any of the "cognitive process elements" and the more tangible "components" is, in actuality, complex, idiosyncratic, and continuous.

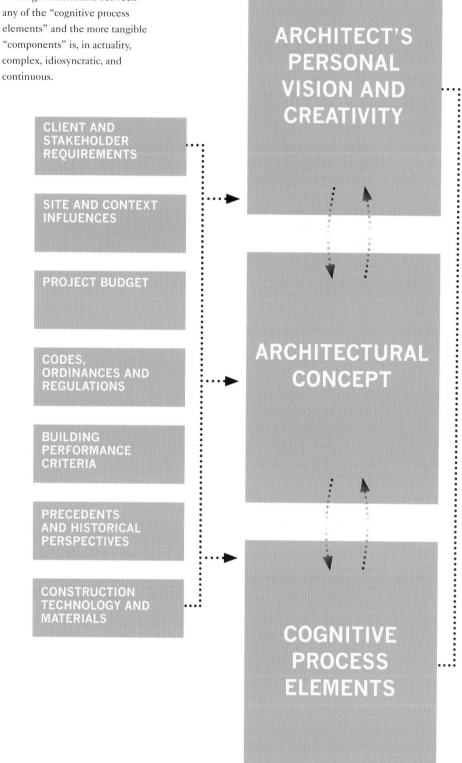

- Tim McGinty cites another example of a great concept suggested in the program for the Carpenter Center of the Visual Arts at Harvard.[17] The program stated that if more students were aware of the activities and life of the center, then they might enroll in courses offered there. The architect, Le Corbusier, translated that concept into a bold physical response. He transformed an existing path on the site into a dramatic public circulation ramp that tunneled through the middle of the building, providing inviting views into many of the studios and workshops.

- The concrete shell vaults of the Sydney Opera House, designed by Jorn Utzon, are an icon for Australia. The concept is one of analogy: The powerful forms interpret and caricature the sailboats and waves of the surrounding Sydney Harbour.

Figure 1.3 is a diagrammatic summary of the contributants to concept and design. It must be emphasized that nothing depicted here is the result of a linear flow of events or ideas. Process elements and personal vision variables infuse each component and serially feed back upon an architectural concept and ultimately to the emerging design. It is no accident that this diagram resembles those depicting theories of cognition. Architectural design is a specialized form of information processing, problem solving, and behavior in the face of the unknown, all of which are, as cognitive psychologists point out, vastly undetermined by experimental evidence. One thing common to most representations of cognition, inclusive of my own modest effort in the architectural realm, are what amount to the rather self-evident input and context nodes (components) and output, which in the present model equals cognitive process elements and emerging design.

Formulating an essential question or proposition—a "thesis"—about what it is you want to accomplish with the design of a particular project is another way to gain insight into the underlying rationale of a concept. One beguiling aspect about design is that there is never *one* perfect question—or *one* ideal answer! However, every thesis must also pass critical scrutiny and professional rigor (more on this later in Chapter 3 in "Seeking dialogue and criticism"). A good thesis clearly sets forth the architect's compass (and position). Like any good thesis it ought to be clear, provocative, and amenable to modification. Examples of good thesis statements are:[18]

- Venturi's work is based on his belief that modern architecture failed to satisfy the public due to its lack of readily understandable symbolism.

- McDonough asserts that contemporary architecture is unsuccessful because it fails to meaningfully respond to the physical environment within which it is situated.

Each of these two thesis statements allows the architect to make the leap to a theme or concept that supports design exploration and expression. One can almost picture the array of resultant forms that are called for and animated by these statements. The thesis can be viewed then, in academic terms, as a heuristic that guides and focuses a design response to a problem. And, the design process itself, in turn, can be understood as a heuristic method or general strategy for solving a problem.

A variation on the thesis statements above is the design thesis, most commonly used to satisfy requirements for a Masters project in architecture school. Here is a design thesis by Nicholas Reisen[19] that resulted in a fine investigation: "Infill residences can be models of sustainability while contributing to the history of their location."

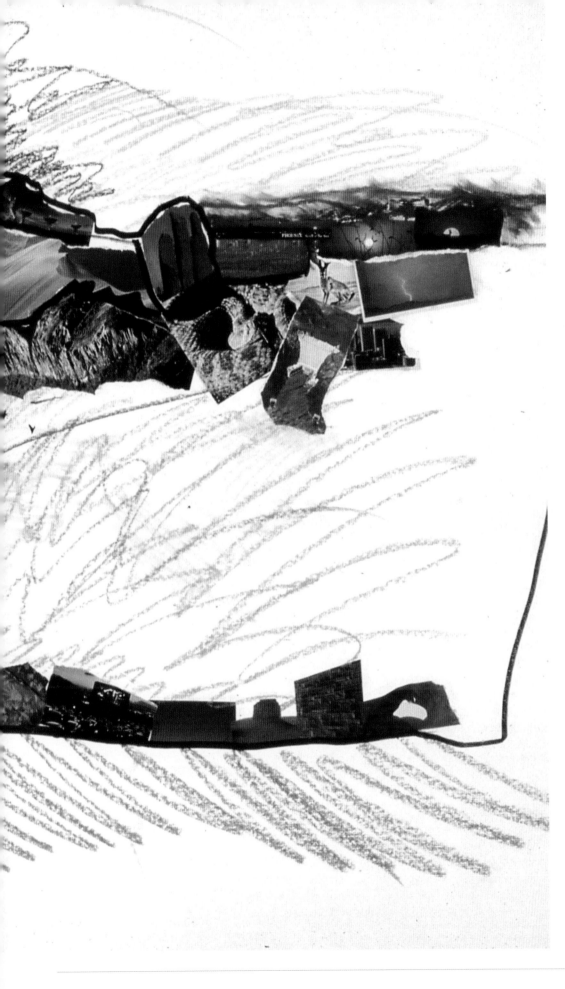

Figure 1.4
Collage for the design of the
Arizona Science Center, Phoenix,
AZ. The overriding site conditions
of silhouette and backlight are
described in the collage. The
design blends influences from
geological events with site-specific
concerns and urban opportunities
(Antoine Predock Architect PC).

Another design thesis by Noreen Richards,[20] which is more resolved and site-specific but equally effective at yielding an excellent design outcome, follows:

> Through the introduction of horticultural and other bioclimatic systems, mid-rise commercial buildings can become supporters and generators of life. These mono-functional, energy-intensive, ubiquitous, and often uninspired elements of the urban landscape can be reconceived as centers for economic activity, social vitality and experiential enjoyment. This effort will focus on one such building located in Albuquerque, New Mexico to serve as a prototype, developing a design approach that can be applied across the typology. In this way, the proposed intervention has potential impact beyond one building or one city.

Thinking about the use of a design thesis toward creation of an architectural concept is analogous to reflecting on the question, "What do you want to say?" when writing is the medium. Janet Emig[21] has observed that scholars and experimentalists such as Vygotsky, Luria, and Bruner have all declared that the thought process that leads to writing incorporates analysis and synthesis, and by definition can be seen as heuristic. She has further suggested that any form of composing, such as composing a painting, a symphony, a dance, a film, or *a building*, can be construed as employing distinct but related cognitive strategies.

Thus, while not necessarily a new idea, understanding the process of developing a design thesis as a heuristic in service of an architectural concept may be a valuable approach to demystifying design. While calling for a dedicated, specific exploration, this line of reasoning may also suggest the utility of the process we use in architecture as a tool for problem solving in broader contexts.

Recapitulating, inspiration for concepts can be derived from many project-specific sources as well as from a personal vision, or some combination thereof. Concepts can emerge from a careful analysis of attributes of the site and its context including the culture, traditions, history, landscape, etc.; or from the program, including client requirements, preferences, budget, the vision and mission of the enterprise, and precedents of similar building types; or from construction technology and building performance goals; and so on. Structural expression, materials selections and applications, building systems, and craft should, ideally, all be considered early in the design process to stimulate generation of multiple design concepts. Developing a concept is an opportunity to think broadly and abstractly about conditions underlying and surrounding a project, not solely in practical terms. Interviewed in the *New York Times* in 2006, Daniel Libeskind illuminates his personal search for ideas, describing his design modus operandi: "I put myself in the spirit of the place. My goal is to invent something memorable that isn't obvious, but is connected to the roots of the place."[22]

Antoine Predock's position on "reinventing place" is similar to Libeskind's. He says: "It is our job, our responsibility to draw out unknown qualities, perhaps those that form the essence of the place that formerly may not have been understood in the most complete way."[23] Predock's design process includes creating a collage of images related to specific site attributes. For example, the Arizona Science Center "suggests an assemblage of abstract land forms—peaks, valleys, canyons, mesas—that begin to take form in the collage" (see Figure 1.4).

To transcend mere building and create something beyond a design's immediate utility (i.e., a culturally significant work of art), Christopher Mead, Professor of Architecture and of Art History at the University of New Mexico, underscores the importance of formulating "a project's aesthetic and social purpose at the start, so that the project as it develops can constantly be measured against this original conception."[24] Moreover, the best ideas (and their built expression) are widely accessible—legible and understandable—to all, not just to the cognoscenti. The creative leap (and there must be a creative leap)—doing something innovative, inspired, or poetic—means that project information has been thoughtfully gathered, considered, and synthesized appropriately for the circumstance. It doesn't necessarily translate to an avant-garde, unconventional solution.

A service-oriented and client-driven sensibility is absolutely necessary but—equally absolute—that sensibility alone is not sufficient to create architecture. AIA Gold-Medalist Thom Mayne, FAIA believes that the best work arises from a continuum of research and exploration from one's life and career experience. Raising the design bar can be a natural consequence of that experience. The challenge, then, is reconciling a personal vision with the specific demands of a project including the pragmatics of program and budget. Now is the time to demonstrate to the client in compelling fashion what is possible, what the client could never have imagined. Mayne succinctly emphasizes the point: "Bringing to bear something outside the pragmatic engenders architecture."[25] It will become clear that the design process is a powerful mechanism for creatively solving problems.

Having noted that which is outside the pragmatic, I hasten to add that service and art are not mutually exclusive goals. Renzo Piano, in his Pritzker Architecture Prize acceptance speech of 1998, described an approach to service:

> Listening to people is important. And this is especially difficult for an architect. Because there is always the temptation to impose one's own design, one's own way of thinking or, even worse, one's own style. I believe, instead, that a light approach is needed. Light, but without abandoning the stubbornness that enables you to put forward your own ideas whilst being permeable to the ideas of others.[26]

Is it more courageous to listen and respond to the client, or to remain unyielding in standing behind some ideal creation? Perhaps it is this very tension between practical exigencies and ideals that motivates innovation and keeps creativity tied to the solution of mundane but often significant challenges.

Design process as research

The proposition that design is a form of research has been and continues to be a controversial discussion. Broadly construed, research can be viewed as a systematic means of developing answers to questions. As a process, there is a standardized set of procedures or at least a semblance of rigor and integrity in a method of inquiry and analysis of outcomes. While not excluding spontaneity, there is little question that capricious, fanciful, or arbitrary thinking has no place in research process or product.

Usually in response to some form of question or problem, a disciplined collection of various kinds of data is undertaken, followed by interpretation and synthesis toward, in the case of architecture, a three-dimensional outcome. Both the process and result, therefore, appear phenomenologically similar to research protocol and product.

It is not a stretch, then, to suggest that the outcomes of architectural design serve as experiments through which concepts are developed, transformed into buildings, then critically evaluated in terms of function, performance, and aesthetic success.

The notion of design as a variation on experimental scientific method encompassing observation and hypothesis testing through experimentation may not be so far-fetched. The utility of this notion may lie in how we as architects habitually braid theory and practice toward innovation across various building types. Beyond achieving academic parity with more mainstream research disciplines, design as research is a construct that may genuinely be an effective cognitive strategy for interrogating our buildings, i.e., "is this particular scheme for a state-of-the-art library successful and generalizable to other similar libraries?" Assume that the "scheme" here is the answer to a set of complex questions requiring multiple dimensions of data gathering and novel, previously untested synthesis leading to a built result. Thus, research processes drive or underlie the design process, and the result itself is "research." The logical extension of the reasoning here is that design is merely a distinct subset of research, and finally then, that architecture is a research discipline.

Notes

0.   Antoine Predock, interview by the author, Albuquerque, NM, December 18, 1999.

1.   Screenplay by Woody Allen and Marshall Brickman, "Annie Hall," *Four Films of Woody Allen*, New York: Random House, 1982, p. 40.

2.   Antoine Predock, interview by the author, Albuquerque, NM, December 18, 1999.

3.   Tim Brown, "Design Thinking," *Harvard Business Review* vol. 86 no. 6, June 2008, 88–89.

4.   Bradford Perkins, FAIA, "Design Phases," *The Architect's Handbook of Professional Practice*, Fourteenth Edition, Hoboken, NJ: John Wiley & Sons, 2008, p. 522.

5.   Don Metz, *Confessions of a Country Architect*, Piermont, NH: Bunker Hill Publishing, 2007, p. 101.

6.   Antoine Predock, interview by the author, Albuquerque, NM, December 18, 1999.

7.   Thom Mayne, interview by the author, Albuquerque, NM, June 8, 2000.

8.   Merrill Elam, interview by Heather Livingston, *AIA Architect*, May 30, 2008.

9.   Shirley Blumberg, panel discussion, "Recapturing lost territories," *Inform 2006: number two*, p. 8.

10. Clark Kellogg, "Focus on the Future: Learning from Studio," *Design Intelligence Knowledge Reports*, January 2006, p. 9.

11. Michael Maltzan, "Trajectory of Change: An Interview with Michael Maltzan," *National Building Museum Online*, July and August 2008.

12. Twyla Tharp, "Creativity Step by Step: A Conversation with Choreographer Twyla Tharp," *Harvard Business Review* vol. 86 no. 4, April 2008, 50.

13. Tim Brown, "Design Thinking," *Harvard Business Review* vol. 86 no. 6, June 2008, 87.

14. Bryan Lawson, *How Designers Think: The Design Process Demystified*, Fourth Edition, Oxford: Architectural Press, 2006, p. 273.

15. Norman Weinstein, "Artful Writing," *The Chronicle of Higher Education*, http://chronicle.com, vol. 54 issue 26, March 7, 2008, B21.

16. Anne Taylor, *Linking Architecture and Education: Sustainable Design of Learning Environments*, Albuquerque: University of New Mexico Press, 2009, p. 3.

17. Tim McGinty, *Introduction to Architecture*, New York: McGraw-Hill, 1979, p. 208.

18. From Indiana University, Center for Design Process, http://www.indiana.edu/~iucdp/thesis.html.

19. Nicholas Reisen, courtesy of his faculty advisor Professor Mark Childs, personal communication with the author, May 22, 2010.

20. Noreen Richards, courtesy of her faculty advisors Professors Mark Childs and Kuppu Iyengar, personal communication with the author, June 12, 2010.

21. Janet Emig, "Writing as a Mode of Learning," *College Composition and Communication* vol. 28 no. 2, May 1977, 122–28.

22. Daniel Libeskind, interview by Edward Lewine, the *New York Times Magazine*, May 21, 2006, p. 41.

23. Antoine Predock, interview by the author, Albuquerque, NM, December 18, 1999.

24. Christopher Mead, quoted by the author in "It's not personal, it's business: Peer review and self-criticism are crucial tools that elevate the quality of preliminary designs," *Architectural Record* vol. 187 no. 9, September 1999, 28.

25. Thom Mayne, interview by the author, Albuquerque, NM, June 8, 2000.

26. Renzo Piano was awarded the Pritzker Architecture Prize from President Bill Clinton at a ceremony at the White House on June 17, 1998.

Chapter 2
Influences and inspiration

This chapter focuses on the components of the design process—
including the program, site, context, budgets, codes, precedents,
construction technology, and so on—and how to understand their
potential impact on building design. Even though seemingly
mundane, after careful analysis they may inspire design thinking
and direction. In any case, responding to the array of data specific
to the project components will ensure that the building is well
suited for its intended use in its intended location.

The systematic investigation of environmental variables (i.e., ecological, geological, climatic, and other site conditions and patterns) yields crucial data. Together with social factors (i.e., client and user needs and preferences), a full and project-specific set of challenges and opportunities emerges. Discovering as much raw data as possible at the outset of a project will provide a solid foundation for designing or "processing."

It will become apparent that some of the data-rich information will be developed only after some initial design work. Therefore, testing design ideas or schemes—using them as a means to extract that information and acquire meaningful feedback—is a valuable part of the design process and is the basis for repetition in multiple design loops. This in turn creeps into the realm of construction itself, which necessarily requires an appreciation of construction details and materials. These components must be creatively designed and/or selected in response *to* site and program data—and the architectural concept. As previously discussed, an architectural concept may arise *from* site and program data (for example, see Figure 2.20), and may subsequently be reformulated as further data are elicited or developed. Thus, the apparently ordinary and unimaginative may in fact be much greater than the sum of the constituent parts and lead to the magic of synthesis (which is discussed in Chapter 3).

Clients, stakeholders, and the program

The program is what distinguishes architecture from pure art. The program encompasses project goals; functional requirements, activities, and organizational relationships; client and/or user preferences and aspirations; budgetary factors and limits, construction quality, and schedule; aesthetics and image; response to surrounding context; future needs for expansion, conversion, and phasing capabilities; performance characteristics (i.e., sustainable design features); and all other relevant variables that define clients' and users' needs and preferences.

I hasten to add that the objective programmatic requirements for a building are complemented by the less tangible spirit that underlies the matrix of functional requirements, square footages, and adjacencies. Louis Kahn wrote, regarding his design for Mikveh Israel: "I must be in tune with the spirit that created the first synagogue. I must rediscover that sense of beginnings through beliefs." While reverential about program, Kahn sought what Herbert Muschamp termed the "metaphysical" underpinnings of a building.[1] This additional and admittedly more elusive programmatic feature reflects the architect's understanding of social, cultural, and historical contexts. While Kahn placed a priority on the pragmatic value of "servant" spaces, he simultaneously appreciated that an institution such as a library should not merely be a collection of artfully arranged warehousing for shelving, but should celebrate the life of the mind that these spaces support. Imagine the design responses that such a programmatic statement could evoke.

Graphic expression of the program promotes appreciation of relationships between various functional elements, suggests ideal adjacencies and patterns of use, and may help develop a sense of scale, area, and volumes. Bubble diagrams are abstract graphic representations of the program spaces and their layout (see Figures 2.1 and 2.2 for examples). They offer a fundamental understanding of the program and can certainly facilitate a necessary familiarity with pragmatic and functional issues. However, they can be misinterpreted as an actual architectural solution. If bubble diagrams are taken too literally, a diagrammatic building will result—a building that is an extrusion of the plan. The risk, then, is that bubble diagrams may allow the architect to present a quick fix without taking time to investigate more meaningful underlying ideas or conceptual strategies.

Like most things in life, moderation in use seems to be the key; judicious use of bubble diagrams is an efficient means of exploring the validity of proposed spatial and functional relationships. If they are satisfactory, the paths you trace become circulation diagrams, and represent a rational way to start thinking about organizing spaces.

Bubbles may be drawn in relative scale to each other. Connect related bubbles with lines (use dotted or dashed lines to represent a specific type of relationship [i.e., public versus private]); move them close together to show proximity; use heavy lines to show heavy or frequent traffic flow. If there are too many bubbles, condense those that are closely associated (see Figure 2.3). For example, bedroom, bathroom, and closets may comprise the single bubble representing a master bedroom. Annotate the diagrams to clarify or convey additional information. This sort of documentation can be an effective tool for justifying design decisions to clients.

There are scores of other visual depictions that may be employed. Some demonstrate circulation, showing vehicular, pedestrian, and service movement (see Figures 2.4, 2.5, and 3.36 for more examples); others, such as adjacency matrices, catalog all spaces and categorize the relationships between spaces. For complex programs there are more sophisticated methods for collecting and analyzing data, but these are generally the province of programming consultants.

Throughout the preliminary design phase, discussions with the client and with stakeholders (i.e., building users, neighbors or community group representatives, sponsors, etc.) are invaluable in eliciting information that helps define the problem and provide cues to solve it. Because the client often has difficulty in voicing needs and problems, the architect has an early opportunity to be a creative diagnostician. And, as the design professional, the architect has a responsibility to understand precisely what the client is trying to say. Continuing conversations and diagnoses through the preliminary design phase fine-tune (or in some cases redefine) the program to ensure an optimal design response. Edie Cherry, FAIA,[2] underscores the importance of "active listening," that is, concentrating on what the client says, how they say it, and most importantly, why they say it.

Active listening sets the stage for interpreting information and merging it with professional judgment and ideas into a meaningful architectural design. For example, reference an idea the client either stated, squiggled on the back of a napkin, or showed as a precedent that made its way into the design scheme. Point out how the client's squiggle perhaps triggered an idea, was translated into a plan or physical response, and describe how it was influential in making a design decision (see Figure 2.6). If it represents a genuine contribution, celebrate it, and the client will be that much more invested in the project.

The program can serve as a device for incorporating the input of the client and other stakeholders. Ultimately, better listening and interaction can be promoted, along with rapport. Maintaining an open mind and low-profile ego during the programming process and eliciting and managing appropriate input from all stakeholders can only enhance truly reciprocal communication between architect and client, and will therefore best support client and project interests.

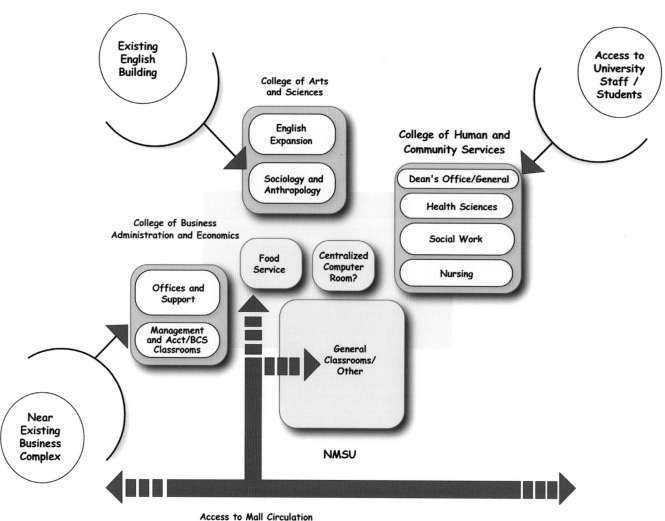

Existing
English
Building

College of Arts
and Sciences

English
Expansion

Sociology and
Anthropology

Access to
University
Staff /
Students

College of Human and
Community Services

Dean's Office/General

Health Sciences

Social Work

Nursing

College of Business
Administration and Economics

Food
Service

Centralized
Computer
Room?

Offices and
Support

Management
and Acct/BCS
Classrooms

General
Classrooms/
Other

Near
Existing
Business
Complex

NMSU

Access to Mall Circulation

Figure 2.1
Master bubble diagram for a
university classroom and laboratory
building including connections to
campus buildings and circulation
routes (Architectural Research
Consultants, Incorporated).

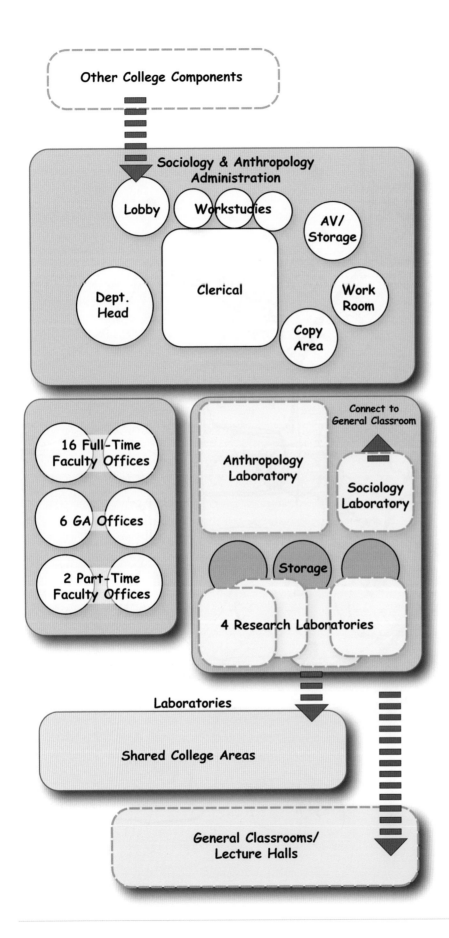

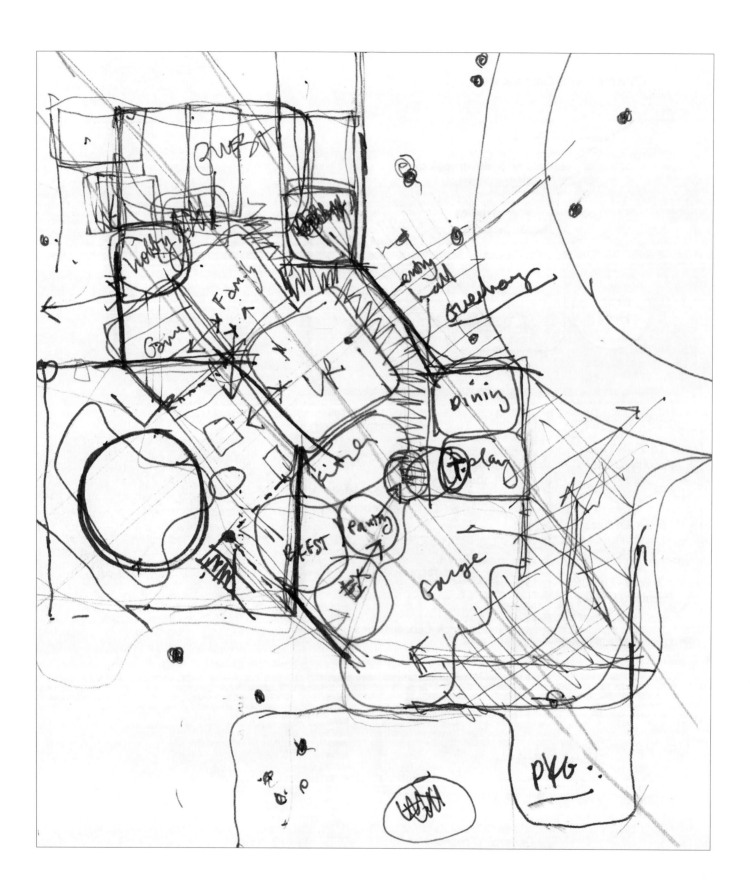

Figure 2.3
In this condensed version of
a bubble diagram for a large
residence in Florida, the bubbles
are drawn at relative scale and
pushed together to emphasize the
importance of spatial adjacencies.

Figure 2.4
Massing diagrams depict the
program elements in three
dimensions, and can illustrate
vertical organizational possibilities
(illustration by Youngsu Lee and
Alissa MacInnes from Alread,
Jason and Thomas Leslie, *Design-
Tech: Building Science for Architects*,
Architectural Press, 2007).

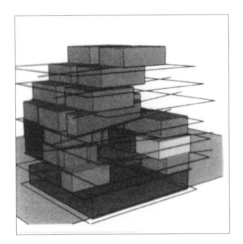 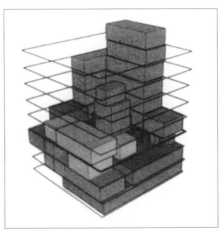 

Figure 2.5
Color-coded and annotated diagrammatic floor plan serving as a visual
depiction of scaled program elements (Michael Dickson/SMPC
Architects).

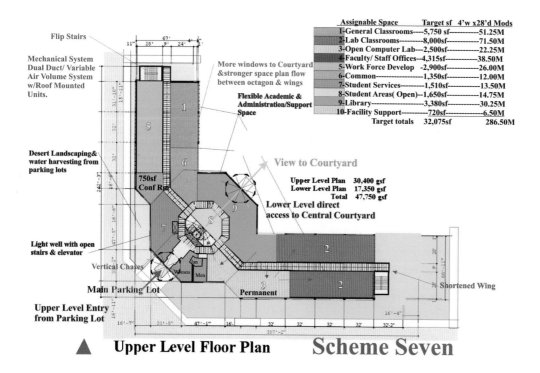

Assignable Space	Target sf	4'w x28'd Mods
1-General Classrooms	5,750 sf	51.25M
2-Lab Classrooms	8,000sf	71.50M
3-Open Computer Lab	2,500sf	22.25M
4-Faculty/ Staff Offices	4,315sf	38.50M
5-Work Force Develop	2,900sf	26.00M
6-Common	1,350sf	12.00M
7-Student Services	1,510sf	13.50M
8-Student Areas(Open)	1,650sf	14.75M
9-Library	3,380sf	30.25M
10-Facility Support	720sf	6.50M
Target totals	32,075sf	286.50M

Flip Stairs

Mechanical System
Dual Duct/ Variable
Air Volume System
w/Roof Mounted
Units.

More windows to Courtyard
&stronger space plan flow
between octagon & wings

Flexible Academic &
Administration/Support
Space

Desert Landscaping&
water harvesting from
parking lots

View to Courtyard

750sf
Conf Rm

Upper Level Plan   30,400 gsf
Lower Level Plan   17,350 gsf
          Total   47,750 gsf

Lower Level direct
access to Central Courtyard

Light well with open
stairs & elevator

Vertical Chases

Main Parking Lot

Shortened Wing

Upper Level Entry
from Parking Lot

Permanent

▲ **Upper Level Floor Plan**   **Scheme Seven**

Drawing diagrams on yellow trace or on a computer—in front of the client, either one-on-
one or in a workshop setting—can be an effective strategy to advance the dialogue about
space requirements and relationships (see Figure 2.7). Sometimes, communicating the
essence of complex ideas to clients can be best accomplished with a hand-drawn napkin
sketch.

Much of what I've been discussing is about effective communication—a way of eliciting
"data" *from* clients and of presenting architectural responses *to* clients. Architects who
believe that great communication, together with a genuine service ethic is important, have
satisfied clients who provide repeat commissions and referrals. Very few clients want to
engage an architect who is interested only in his or her own aesthetic sensibilities. It is
unlikely that a brilliant solitary designer who doesn't have an attitude of reciprocity—like
the malignantly narcissistic Howard Roark character in *The Fountainhead*—would be a
respected professional. And again, what may distinguish architecture from pure art is the
satisfaction inherent in addressing specific needs, rather than simply serving the architect's
inner muse. Reconciling diverse and conflicting perspectives into a bold design scheme,
while building consensus, can be enormously gratifying.

Working with building committees
Building committees are formed to represent the interests of the client and stakeholders
on institutional, civic, educational, and other project types. How should architects deal

Figure 2.6
(top) Client-sketched floor
plan; (bottom) Translation of
client's sketch to a schematic
plan (Andrew Pressman, FAIA
and Siegel Design, Architects).

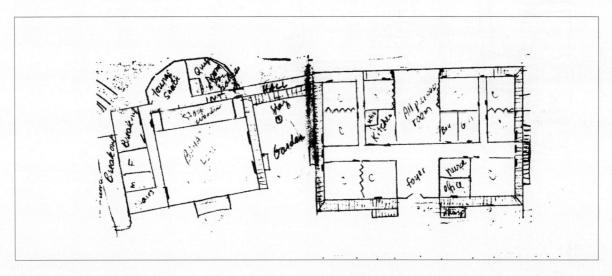

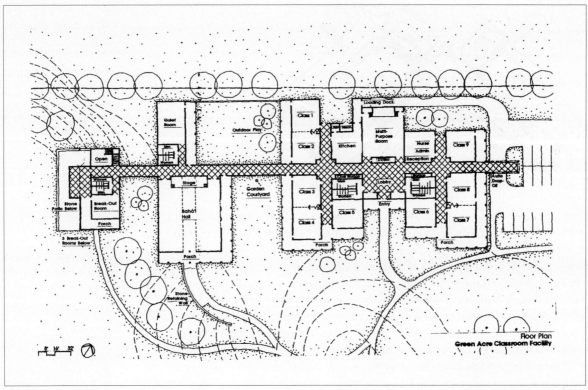

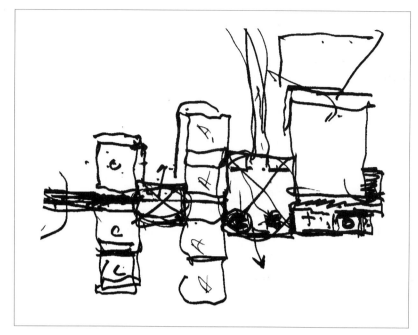

Figure 2.7
(top) Space analysis for a classroom and public meeting facility drawn with the client during a presentation; (bottom) Diagram focusing on the major programmatic organizing elements of a clinic used to affirm the client's notion of two distinct groupings of spaces.

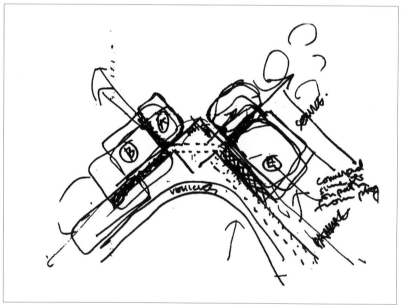

with committees to enhance the process of creating excellent buildings? It is the architect's personal relationship with committee members that can reach beyond bureaucratic politics that tend to grind design projects toward mediocrity and sameness. There is certainly no formula for engaging committees but a genuine concern for client needs, particularly in the programming phase, is obviously crucial to the success of any project. However, responsiveness to what stakeholders want or need should not be used as an excuse for poor design work. Great design transcends the program.

Unfortunately, most architects have little or no formal education in group dynamics, negotiation, or working in teams. But, to succeed at committee-based architectural design, architects must at least be willing to strive to become skilled performers, collaborators, psychologists, arbitrators, and facilitators.

There are several factors to consider in order to productively engage building committees. Architect Kent Larson[3] has much experience with committees and observes the following: (1) *Motivations vary*. Understanding why each person joined a committee is the first step in working successfully with the group. (2) *Skills and interests are very different*. Some members have only pragmatic planning concerns, some are interested only in controlling the money, and some are bored with anything but aesthetic issues. (3) *The path of least resistance is banality*. Strong ideas will elicit powerful emotional responses pro and con. Weak design work is the easiest to get a committee to approve. (4) *Prima donnas don't go far with committees*. While it is important to keep a design from being undermined, it is the kiss of death to become labeled as an unsympathetic artist who is unconcerned with the needs and wishes of the client. An architect should cultivate working relationships with the people of influence on a committee. And (5) *Pick the battles*. Consider accepting a few inappropriate suggestions if they do not affect the core elements of a design.

From a project's inception, the building committee (and architect) must be fully cognizant of the committee's explicit charge and its power, i.e., does it function in an advisory capacity only? Does a board of directors, city council, or some other authority consider its recommendations? Edie Cherry[4] emphasizes that it is not wise to let a group believe they have more decision-making authority than they really have, because if their decision is overridden at a higher level, they may feel betrayed by the architect or facilitator.

Interviewing clients and stakeholders
Interviews with clients and stakeholders can reveal much about a project along the spectrum from abstract and theoretical to practical. Successful interviews can assist in acquiring a full understanding of the client, how and why the project came into being, what the building is truly about, how it should ideally function, and its relationship to the community. Some of this information may even be necessary to prepare a compelling proposal to secure the commission. Most of this information is necessary as a prerequisite to developing preliminary schemes. However, there will still be a number of programmatic unknowns that will only be discovered as the design progresses.

There is simply no substitute for getting out in the field and gathering "data." Ask questions about what people want—and what they don't want. Review the proposed program and elicit suggestions for improvement and development of the program. Take time to share your vision, and you are bound to get a great deal in return. Try to appreciate the stakeholders' unique perspectives.

Effective assessment requires personal contact and connection. Discover the value of what is being said between the lines, then check it out. Test any hypotheses you may form simply by asking: "Does this make sense?" Try to take notes privately; reflect after you've left the site. Writing while someone is taking the time to talk with you may be experienced as distancing or rude.

Do not neglect social or community factors. Talk to influential people in the neighborhood. If appropriate or possible, solicit opinions in the local park or grocery store. Elicit reactions to the possibility of a prospective project. Buy a local newspaper—be aware of pressing problems and the political exigencies in the area. Observe what is happening during the day and night, and note what seems positive together with what seems negative. Record your thoughts.

It is conventional wisdom that sensitivity to community input will not only promote the ultimate success of a project, but will likely enhance the probability of approvals from any design review boards, public agencies, associations, or planning boards that have authority to approve designs.

Always recall the cautionary note about moderation: Much tangential information is bound to result from inquiries and discussions. Try to avoid preoccupation with irrelevant factors, however colorful they may be. Keep the big picture in clear focus. And remain alert to valuable bits of information that may emerge spontaneously from conversations with stakeholders.

The medical model for interviewing can be applied to architecture to help define and understand the project. A good interview is one in which stated problems are clarified, and unstated problems are discovered and given voice. A level of "diagnostic" understanding is achieved, and this points the way toward optimal design. Attempt to establish a trusting alliance with the client; little if anything of value will ensue without trust. If there is such a thing as the standard condition for engaging people, it is rapport. To have rapport with another, be yourself; you should neither affect some wooden formality you may believe is "professional" nor be excessively casual and familiar. And the client's perception that at some level he or she is being *cared for* will likely enhance participation, the quality of information offered, and wishes voiced.

Another strategy for successfully engaging clients is to maintain a sense of humor. Steve Martin's[5] observation of Carl Reiner as a film director is a great model: "He had an entrenched sense of glee; he used humor as a gentle way of speaking difficult truths; and he could be effortlessly frank."

In order to guide the diagnostic encounter with the client toward maximizing efficiency, take some time before the initial meeting to form some specific hypotheses about what the current clients and building users want and need. Utilize these notions to shape probing and questioning either to confirm or reject your ideas. Confirmation of hypotheses allows you the luxury of eliciting valuable details, and rejection of expectations immediately sets up questioning designed to discover new facts that will in turn support alternative concepts.

Here is a simple example of the benefits of architect–client dialogue. Consider an office project. If the architect invests the time to make him or herself visible and well known as an active listener, he or she is likely to be seen as an employee advocate. This situation may even enhance morale: Not only are employee needs given voice, but there is personal investment in the design process. Another less obvious question to explore is: How do clients perceive and engage the office? Meet with representative clients. This may not only reveal another point of view and stimulate new concepts, but may serve to deepen existing relationships and add to the firm's service reputation. Another example: Following discussions with management and employees, desired conference rooms are projected as underutilized. The architect is in a position to suggest a dual function: Meeting room and employee lounge. With careful scheduling, multipurpose utilization can save space and cost. So, maximize the participatory element; enlist people connected with the project as collaborators. Promise only what you know you can deliver.

It may be helpful to identify and formally recognize select stakeholders as collaborators who can enrich the design process at the outset of a project, when their input can be most consequential. An investment of time early on—whether through workshop, charrette (see Chapter 3), or one-on-one conversations—to glean insights about the program, client operations, and activities will likely reduce time in later phases due to fewer design questions and changes.

"Design excellence and social responsibility are inextricably connected." This quote from James Stewart Polshek, FAIA,[6] perfectly describes our obligation as design professionals to serve both the interests of clients and to maintain a transcendent social responsibility. James Timberlake, FAIA,[7] echoed this sentiment in accepting the 2008 AIA Architecture Firm Award. He stated: "We can no longer be content with creating simple shelter or thrilling form.... It is our responsibility to fight for those that live in substandard conditions, in failing and nonexistent infrastructure, and to confront the tremendous impact that architecture makes on the carbon footprint of the world." Do not necessarily accept a list of program functions at face value; identify opportunities to make more socially responsive environments. Architects have a pedagogical responsibility to broaden clients' perspectives about the built environment. Clients may be somewhat myopic; they may not be aware of greater possibilities, which do not necessarily translate to inflation of the construction budget or increasing the scope of work. Be prepared to "sell" unconventional ideas to clients; back them up with facts and observations from your perspective as an expert. Being persuasive often simply amounts to illuminating a well-studied idea.

Site and context

Always design a thing by considering it in its next larger context—a chair
in a room, a room in a house, a house in an environment, an environment
in a city plan.

Eliel Saarinen[8]

At every scale, the site literally and figuratively connects architecture to the larger world. The site is such an essential part of evaluating opportunities and constraints at the outset of a project that even before design begins, its very location and character may determine whether a project is viable, and subsequently will influence many design decisions. At the very least, the site is one point at which the heavy lifting of design may begin. Consider variables that are relevant at the regional scale, including history, culture, natural material resources, and all types of infrastructure such as transportation networks, power and water supplies, telecommunications, schools, and community services. Working from regional down to site scales, systematic analysis changes focus to local context including climate, environmental, and geological conditions, vegetation, surrounding buildings, and so on.

Architect Yoshio Taniguchi[9] said in a *New York Times Magazine* interview: "The site is the point of departure, the most basic issue in architecture." He asserted that actually visiting the site helps him to avoid a natural tendency to be seduced by the latest abstract theory or idiosyncratic vision.

Incorporation of site issues into design is fundamental to achieving excellence. The emphasis today on green and sustainable design is noble but perhaps analogous to reinventing the wheel. Good architecture has always been defined by an active engagement with, and response to, a constellation of site factors: Topography, solar path, wind, vegetation, climate, views, context, preservation of natural site amenities, and so on—all by definition "green."

Every site and its context is made up of a unique mosaic of attributes and environmental forces (see Figure 2.8). The spectacular, the mundane, and even the bleak characteristics of a proposed site must be systematically noted and analyzed, and considered as factors that will influence the architecture. This is where the *place* of place making originates. The relationship of building and site (i.e., integration and harmony) is extremely important in attaining design excellence. Both Malcolm Wells and Cesar Pelli—representing fairly diverse theoretical positions—share a similar sentiment. (Wells:[10] "Improve the land when you build, or don't build there." Pelli:[11] "We should not judge a building by how beautiful it is in isolation, but instead by how much better or worse that particular place has become by its addition.")

Figure 2.8
Three contrasting sites, left to right: Southwest desert artists' colony, tropical paradise, and dense urban high-rises represent very different contexts that suggest unique architectural responses.

Indeed, zooming out from buildings to places acknowledges that designing a building presents an opportunity to enrich the experience of its larger context. Hismen Hin-Nu Terrace, a mixed-use development in Oakland, California, does just that with vending stalls built into the front of the structure. Designed by Pyatok Architects, the project actively engages the street, contributing to the vitality, safety, and redevelopment of the neighborhood. Improving the public realm, the quality of city life, should be part of the conversation in developing almost every project.

Appreciating the environment

In the introduction to *Design with Nature*, the classic text by Ian McHarg, Lewis Mumford[12] succinctly restates the timeless wisdom of Hippocrates: "Man's life, in sickness and in health, is bound up with the forces of nature, and that nature, so far from being opposed and conquered, must rather be treated as an ally and friend, whose ways must be understood, and whose counsel must be respected." Especially today, few would dispute that thoughtful responses to the environment help tie a building to its site, conserve energy, and may contribute to the preservation of vital ecologies. What may be less evident is that an intimate knowledge of the site can electrify design concepts. How does one become intimate with the site? Start with a simple walk-through. Then, spend a few hours at the site at different intervals throughout the day, over a period of time to uncover the dynamic events—both natural and human-made. Ideally, one would camp there for a year to get a sense of the inherent rhythms, cycles, and patterns. Notwithstanding taking a sabbatical to do that, plan on as many trips as possible during the course of the project, as the design develops.

Antoine Predock[13] has stressed the importance of understanding the natural context over time. He says architects must "sit on a site, put their butts on the ground, feeling and sensing the spirit of the place." Predock suggests that his sensitivity to site is due in part to living in New Mexico, a place where "the geological presence is palpable. Your feet feel time. You can sense the land moving through your body." I would add that an urban site is no less dynamic and evocative. In any case, go to the site before breakfast and have dinner at the coffee shop across the street. Walk your dog on the site. The goal is to log some quality time there and in the grass, the dirt, and the neighborhood, and imagine possibilities and constantly test design ideas.

Illustrations of site influences on design

Vegetation. A lush, wooded site may suggest a particular architectural expression. Pinecote, the Crosby Arboretum Interpretive Center designed by Fay Jones, FAIA, takes a cue from the surrounding Mississippi pine savannah. Jones[14] has said: "The time of day and the seasonal changes modify the shadows that frame the light. The edges of the roof are not crisp at all. Like the pine straw and pine limbs, they progressively thin out from something that's close and dense to something open and fragile." Design concepts can indeed emerge from the natural qualities of the site.

Climate. Solar: Optimize building orientation and massing for local heating and cooling conditions. Configure fenestration, overhangs, and other devices to allow penetration of low winter sun and block high summer sun; consider thermal characteristics when selecting cladding materials; design forms consistent with renewable energy strategies (i.e., photovoltaic arrays); harvest and control the quality of day lighting; consider using deciduous trees that can help filter sun in summer and allow penetration of sunlight in winter. Evergreens, of course, provide a year-round barrier. In tropical latitudes, tall palms can provide shade without blocking cool breezes at window level.

Wind: Orient and shelter entries to mitigate the bite of cold winter winds; capture summer breezes for ventilation of indoor spaces and outdoor areas. Remember that the force of wind produces a variety of stresses and strains, which can lift the roof off a house or cause tall buildings to sway. These potential stresses, together with wind patterns and prevailing wind direction, must always be considered for a particular location and factored into the design.

Rain: Avoid siting buildings in low areas with a history of flooding (or without some sort of control system); evaluate water runoff from paved and built areas (see Figure 2.13). Consider possibilities for harvesting and storing rainwater for domestic, irrigation, or greywater uses. Glenn Murcutt elegantly expresses rainwater drainage details. For example, in his Magney House, Bingie Point, New South Wales, the gutter and downpipe are extended beyond the exterior wall to create a gateway to the entrance. Murcutt has celebrated water movement in a museum in Kempsey in the profile of the helically fabricated round downpipe, which suggests how water flows in the tube.

Arthur Erickson's Fire Island house is a good example of a building attuned to the exigencies of a climate influenced by salt air and intense beachfront light. The house is finished in cedar boards, which resist corrosion. When the beach is empty and the light low, hinged fences, which are attached to the deck, can be lowered. When they are upright, the bright reflected light is blocked, and a degree of privacy is insured.

Topography. A steep slope may suggest a multilevel scheme and zoning of functions by level with interesting three-dimensional potential. With a steep slope, there may well be accessibility issues. Consider slender forms that align with contours to minimize cutting and filling and disruption to the site, or consider breaking out smaller scale individual program elements to engage the slopes and produce interesting outdoor spaces. It almost goes without saying that a flat site is more amenable to plans based on regular geometric patterns; construction is generally more economical than on steep sites.

A notable example of how a design responds to slope is the Portland, Maine Museum of Art by architect Henry Cobb of Pei Cobb Freed & Partners. Behind its oversized but thin front facade, the building visually steps down a long, sloping site through a series of distinct masses. This scheme underscores the natural dynamics of the slope while helping the new building to relate more easily to the smaller scale of two historic museum buildings that sit at the base of the site. The discrete masses of the new museum serve to house a sequence of galleries designed from cube-like modules. The articulation of the roof and elevation as the museum drops down the slope seems also to amplify the perception of natural light; a series of octagonal lantern skylights yield illumination likened by critics to that achieved in Kahn's late museums. The overall effect is an interesting, functional, modern building that gently complements a challenging site and resonates with modest and unremarkable context.

Actually exploiting a sloping site in direct support of programmatic objectives may also result in an effective design. The public library in Great Neck, New York, by architects Gibbons and Heidtmann is just such a design. A basement level facing a large pond can be entered only from the lowest part of the site. This effectively separates the main public library (at the top of the slope) from the basement level, which is used as a youth center. A special advantage of this scheme is that it allows use of the youth center when the library is closed. Thus, the site is incorporated as a natural zoning device.

Sensory insults: Noise, smells, and bad views. Provide buffer zones (and distance, if possible) to dissipate the problem; thoughtfully select materials (i.e., a translucent material such as glass block, to let in daylight and blur the view). Special construction detailing and materials can help a lot toward acoustical separation, for example.

Barker, Rinker, Seacat & Partners designed a recreation center in Denver's industrial fringe. While the region is known for its beauty, strident local features such as a commercial strip development, an oil refinery, warehousing, and a dog track presented decidedly negative site characteristics. The architects responded by designing an inwardly focused building with exterior sweeps of translucent glass block. The block allows penetration of sunlight while effectively muting the frankly bad views. Interior window walls and a sky-lit atrium help make the recreation center a genuine oasis.

Sensory delights: Good views. Consider sight lines both to and from the site; study what is appropriate relative to the design concept. Frame views from the site to heighten drama, or configure building elements to mediate views to specific areas.

Josh Schweitzer's weekend retreat is sited in the dramatic (and sometimes seismic) landscape of Joshua Tree, California. It is a spare structure from which one can, without distraction, become immersed in the beauty and rawness of the desert. The essence of the retreat lies in its windows: Meticulously placed, eccentrically cut, and breathtakingly effective at framing views of mountains and desert from the site.

Shepley Bulfinch Richardson and Abbott's Sackler Gallery and National Museum of African Art provides a good example of the control of views *to* a building. In response to pressures to conserve open space at the Smithsonian, 96 percent of the museum was located underground. Three entry pavilions represent the only aboveground structure. The effect is not only to preserve an expansive quadrangle, but also to maintain views to the emblematic essence of the Smithsonian—the original iconic Castle designed by James Renwick in 1849.

Context. Some kind of circumstance-specific response to surroundings may include massing, materials, composing regulating lines (i.e., fenestration, cornice), siting of the building, extension of existing circulation patterns into the site and building, and so on. The late Herbert Muschamp voiced the mandate: "Architecture should contribute to, rather than fit in with, its surroundings." And, Jean Nouvel,[15] the French architect who won the Pritzker Prize in 2008, commented: "Generally, when you say context, people think you want to copy the buildings around, but often context is contrast." Nouvel believes that a building should be in a "dialogue" with its surroundings. I believe that this dynamic give-and-take is the real key to appreciating a response to context. It is often not enough only to quietly mirror context or "respect" surroundings.

An example of a dynamic response to context—that intensifies a site attribute—is the Visual Arts Center at the College of Santa Fe by Ricardo Legorreta. The blue sky in New Mexico is ubiquitous, and its presence is underscored by colorful exterior balconies, one of which is painted a brilliant blue that frequently dissolves into the same tint of the sky; at certain times, building and sky eerily become one.

This is not to say that unobtrusive and subtle responses to context are inappropriate. Kohn Pedersen Fox Associates' 125 Summer Street, a 300-foot-tall office tower in Boston, is a fine example of quiet and restrained contextual responsiveness. The new office

In general, the mission is to describe the inherent makeup of the project area both objectively and impressionistically (i.e., what are the possibilities and challenges, and what is the spirit of the place?). This checklist can be used as a guide for recording site data and deriving the most from frequent visits.

Start with the big picture

- *Maps.* Find a good map (i.e., U.S. Geological Survey, Sanborn maps for urban contexts, Google Earth, etc.). This is a way to begin assessing regional issues—land use (zoning, adjacent building types), access (the nature of traffic: roads, highways, sidewalks), topography, open space, public transportation, and any other features that are important in the area.

- *History.* Acquire a feel for the history of the jurisdiction and the site. What are the building traditions (i.e., materials, typologies, etc.), and why are they traditions? What are they responding to? Document community services (i.e., religious, shopping, health care).

- *Site impressions.* Spend time and walk the site; take photos and sketch typical scenes and details after you've experienced the gestalt in an undistracted manner. Try to develop a "diagnostic impression" of the community; observe people in public spaces and try to understand what makes the spaces successful or dysfunctional. Draw some conclusions about the value of aesthetic, social, and other visible elements. Know where you are: Always orient or key your position (and any photos or sketches) to the maps.

- *Other factors.* Be aware of anything close to the site that may strongly influence design decisions. Pay particular attention to the immediate context: Buildings and open space, views, smells, sounds, pedestrian traffic, vehicular traffic. (For example, is there a noisy air-handling unit on the roof of the adjacent building? When is the area most congested? Which roads bounding the site have less traffic?) These environmental factors are, collectively, all intrinsic to the site. The gestalt also includes buildings in the neighborhood that can provide valuable cues for the architect in terms of massing, detailing, and materials selections.

Preparation for focusing on the site

- *Documents.* Obtain all available documentation about the site—a scaled site plan, survey, and/or aerial photographs showing boundaries, topography, cardinal points, easements, and so on.

- *Site Plan.* Make multiple copies of the site plan (perhaps at a reduced scale) in preparation for field visits. Observations and notes can then be recorded directly and accurately on the plans.

- *Equipment.* Bring a digital camera with a wide-angle lens, and sketching equipment. Bring a ruler or tape measure; you may want to take and/or confirm specific dimensions and relative locations of various site elements. Bring a compass or handheld wireless device with GPS for orientation.

Record site data

- *Views.* Again, photograph the site. And sketch. Awareness of detail is heightened when you actually draw it. In his wonderful book, *Landscape Architecture* 3rd edn. (McGraw-Hill, 1998), John Simonds instructs: "Get the feel of the land ... look, listen, sense." Capture views approaching the site (by foot and/or car) and looking from the site. Attend to, and highlight details (whatever may be useful, i.e., existing structures, rock formations). Key all snapshots and sketches to the site plan.

- *Microclimate.* Document solar path; determine sun angles at various times of the day, and extrapolate how they change throughout the year. Readily available resources, including *Architectural Graphic Standards* (multiple editions), graphically depict how sun angles vary with time and geographical location (latitude). Get a sense of the altitude (angle above the horizon) and azimuth (surface angle measured from the south–north line).

  Observe shadows and shade patterns from nearby buildings, trees, and other features. Also note potential glare problems from reflections from nearby water or shiny facades of existing buildings. Determine direction (and velocity) of prevailing summer and winter winds. Document any changes to typical wind patterns due to hills, buildings, or dense vegetation.

Note any other pertinent climatological and meteorological data, such as patterns of temperature variation, humidity, precipitation (including monsoons, snowfall, or drought), and hurricanes.

Slopes. Field-verify that the topography indicated on the survey is accurate. Show where the land varies from steep to flat, and note the orientation of any slopes. Sketch a few key cross-sections through the site.

Determine how water runoff relates to the slopes. Try to visit the site during a rainstorm. Document drainage features of all types.

Vegetation and wildlife. Note species of trees—evergreen or deciduous—as well as the density, height, and width of the canopy. Identify all types of ground cover.

Describe the habitats of any creatures great and small living on the site.

Existing objects, materials, and public works. Inventory and describe the condition and approximate sizes of existing items, and confirm this on the plan. Much of this is usually indicated on the survey. Include furniture (i.e., benches, picnic tables); lighting; retaining walls; paving; utilities (electricity, gas, water, sanitary sewers, storm drainage, phone lines—and their capacity for new hook-ups); curbs, steps, ramps, handrails, and fences; and fire and police protection. If there are any structures on the site, they need to be evaluated carefully for possible relationship (incorporation versus demolition) to the proposed new project.

Noise and smells. Acoustic and olfactory variables can be very significant; listen for anything potentially disturbing (i.e., an interstate highway bisects the site, a neighbor is an international airport). Are there signs of pollution (i.e., is the site downwind of a factory with big exhaust stacks)?

Subsurface conditions. Information on subsoil and groundwater conditions and data from percolation tests and borings (investigated and analyzed by geotechnical engineers) determine such things as bearing capacity, suitability for septic tank drainage systems, water runoff characteristics, permeability, location of subsurface water (water table), and risk of erosion. Note the presence of topsoil and its influences on potential planting. These studies are fairly routine, and are usually commissioned by the client, in accordance with typical owner–architect agreements.

Depending on site location, seismic factors may be relevant to the design. Check local codes.

Zoning. Zoning is the legal process by which local government specifies and regulates land use and building type, size, and context. Some items that may need specific consideration include setbacks, yards, maximum lot coverage and building height, off-street parking, floor area ratio (ratio of total floor area to site area), sky exposure plane, and permitted uses. There may be other restrictive covenants. Diagram those regulations that have an effect on the site and design (see "Codes, ordinances, and regulations" in Chapter 2).

Renovation of an existing building or tenant build-out. This provides a somewhat different set of cataloging and documentation duties, although many of those mentioned in the preceding text may still be applicable, especially if an addition or outdoor space is programmed.

If not available, scaled (and most important, dimensioned) as-built floor plans and elevations must be developed (or if available, verified). Note floor-to-ceiling heights, fenestration dimensions, sill heights, door sizes, and so on. Getting on hands and knees to measure a building may be a dirty job, but it has its rewards: You are forced to really see detail. Photography here is critical—missed dimensions (there always are a few) can usually be determined by counting bricks, planks, and the like from a snapshot. Any element with a known modular size can be used to achieve a close estimation of an overall dimension. Also, take a few snapshots with a ruler attached to building components. Existing systems (and all associated components)—mechanical and structural—must be recorded. Check the roof and basement; these may be sites of future development. All this information might be available from the building owner or the local building department.

Be aware of special architectural detailing—craftsmanship and design features worth preserving or responding to—both inside and out.

Miscellaneous. This includes anything else specific to the site and immediate vicinity not mentioned in the preceding text (i.e., proximity to bodies of water, floodplains, mud slides, grazing cows, neighbors' air-conditioning units, final approach to a runway, or how the garbage is removed). Determine if there are plans for future development in the area.

building was set back on an irregularly shaped site, behind two nineteenth-century granite-clad five-storey structures. The principal entrance was inserted in the gap that existed between the two older buildings, matching their height, maintaining the building line, and echoing the classically inspired facade elements.

Traffic. Locate access to parking away from busy streets and intersections. Minimize the number of curb cuts and vehicular and pedestrian conflict (i.e., prevent people and automobile routes from crossing).

This variable is another instance in which there is the first-blush impression of mundane and self-evident, but this is decidedly not the case. A most infamous example of how easy it is *not* to address pedestrian circulation is Tysons Corner, Virginia, near Washington, D.C. A relatively recent and genuinely huge medley of commercial, retail, office, and residential space, Tysons Corner is an archetypal edge city: A high-density, mixed-use development that is not a municipality, although it is sufficiently large and populated to qualify as one.

A score of studies and journalistic accounts have documented that walking is virtually impossible. Tysons Corner sits in a network of two major expressways, two cross-county arteries, vast parking lots and garages, and innumerable on/off ramps. The speed and sound of the cars, trucks, buses, and tractor-trailers alone is intimidating to anyone even considering crossing the street from an office building to a shopping mall. The reality is that to cross the street safely, one has to have a car.

Socio-cultural context. This perhaps most challenging factor may have implications for tweaking the building program to meet community needs. Think about the conditions of a particular user group in a particular place and time. Consider the group's resources, struggles, history, worldview; its hopes and dreams.

James Lee Court, a multifamily housing project in Oakland, California by Pyatok Architects Inc., integrates artworks into the facades representing a variety of ethnic groups in the city. For example: "tile designs inspired by West African house painting grace the front entry arch and act as a cornice on the top floor. Symbols for community and prosperity are incorporated in their patterns," says the Pyatok Architects Website.[16] Concepts such as cultural identity, ego, and sanctuary often go without architectural support as the physical manifestations collide with budgetary constraints, or sadly, with the myopic views of bureaucrats or developers.

Diagramming site data
When the inventory of site data is complete, you can thoughtfully investigate the design implications. One approach is to use copies of the site plan, perhaps in a reduced form, to overlay information collected in the field. One diagram can be designated for each inventory category, or several categories may be condensed into a composite map that might reveal noteworthy patterns. Employ graphic symbols to make it easy to understand at a glance (i.e., show steep grades in dark gray and flat areas in white, with light gray for variations in between). Annotate freely as necessary. Another example of graphically illuminating information is the figure-ground (plan) diagram: Looking at neighborhoods in urban districts, building masses are black and open spaces are white. Diagrams are an integral part of the design process because they not only help to form a rationale for design decisions, but can be used artfully and persuasively in client presentations.
The inventory of site data and its subsequent analysis give coherence to development of the site. Typically, a site inventory is initiated with a small-scale site plan. Identify

Figure 2.9
A superb example of a site analysis diagram, including inventory information together with supporting commentary written in the field on a copy of a site survey (John Simonds, *Landscape Architecture,* 3rd edn., New York: McGraw-Hill, 1998, reproduced with permission of the McGraw-Hill Companies).

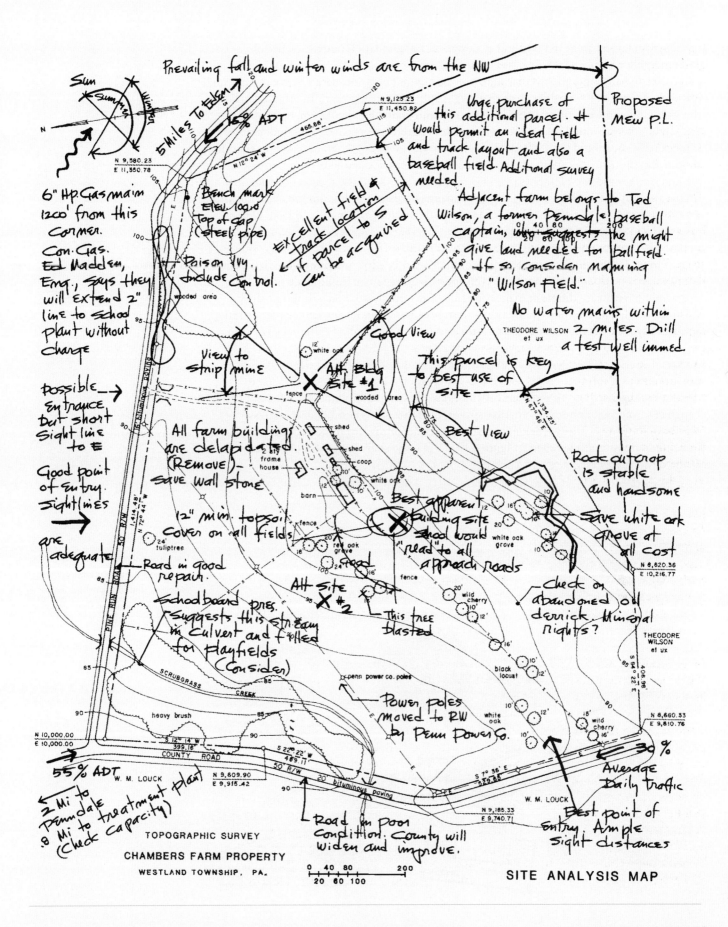

Prevailing fall and winter winds are from the NW

Sun
Summer
Winter

N 9,580.23
E 11,350.78

5 Miles to Etton

15% ADT

N 9,125.23
E 11,450.82

465.86'

N 12° 24' W

Urge purchase of this additional parcel. It would permit an ideal field and track layout and also a baseball field. Additional survey needed.

Proposed NEW P.L.

Adjacent farm belongs to Ted Wilson, a former Penndale baseball captain, who suggests he might give land needed for ballfield. If so, consider naming "Wilson Field."

THEODORE WILSON et ux

No water mains within 2 miles. Drill a test well immed.

6" H.P. Gas main 1200' from this Corner. Con. Gas. Ed Madden, Eng., says they will extend 2" line to school plant without charge

Bench mark Elev. 100.0 Top of Gap (steel pipe)

Excellent field & track location if parcel to S can be acquired

Poison Ivy. Include Control.

wooded area

100

95

View to strip mine

12" white oak

Good View

Att. Bldg Site #1

This parcel is key to best use of site

fence

wooded area

Best View

Good point of Entry. Sight lines are adequate

Possible Entrance but short sight line to E

All farm buildings are delapidated (Remove) — Save Wall stone

12" min. topsoil cover on all fields

shed

shed

coop

2 sty. frame house

white oak

barn

red oak grove

24" tuliptree

Road in good repair.

Schoolboard pres. suggests this stream in culvert and filled for Playfields (Consider)

Alt Site #2

Good

This tree blasted

Best apparent building site. School would "read" to all approach roads

white oak grove

Save white oak grove at all cost

N 8,620.36
E 10,216.77

Rock outcrop is stable and handsome

Check on abandoned oil derrick. Mineral rights?

THEODORE WILSON et ux

wild cherry

fence

black locust

SCRUBGRASS CREEK

heavy brush

penn power co. poles

Power poles moved to RW by Penn Power Co.

white oak

wild cherry

N 8,660.33
E 9,810.76

30%

Average Daily Traffic

N 10,000.00
E 10,000.00

S 12° 14' W
399.16

COUNTY ROAD
50 R/W

N 9,609.90
E 9,915.42

S 22° 22' W
469.11

20' bituminous paving

S 7° 36' E
579.86

Best point of Entry. Ample Sight distances

55% ADT

W. M. LOUCK

2 Mi to Penndale. .8 Mi to treatment plant (Check Capacity)

Road in poor condition. County will widen and improve.

N 9,185.33
E 9,740.71

W. M. LOUCK

TOPOGRAPHIC SURVEY

CHAMBERS FARM PROPERTY

WESTLAND TOWNSHIP, PA.

0 40 80   200
20 60 100

SITE ANALYSIS MAP

(and justify) logical areas to build and to designate for circulation (with cars, people, service, and emergency vehicles). Define areas that ought to be preserved in their natural state, and determine how the integrity of that state may be assured or accentuated by an architectural presence. Conversely, consider areas that might suggest development. In other words, *zone* the site; judge how existing patterns (pedestrian and vehicular circulation, open spaces, etc.) should be extended to and through the site. Is there a pre-existing natural focus of some sort? If so, should it be left alone, framed, or developed? Observations from spending time at the site will almost automatically address these issues and likely raise others that are crucial. It is the site elements that may give clues and have the greatest impact on shaping and orienting the building and supporting circulation. John Simonds,[17] in *Landscape Architecture*, makes the case for harmonizing both the natural and man-made site elements toward the synthesis of a "pleasing" landscape.

Experiment with multiple interpretations of the data. Location and orientation have such an influence on the architecture that, given the same program, a building on one side of a site would have a very different expression than if it were located on a different side. It is interesting and useful to predict the differences in design responses (i.e., fenestration, zoning of spaces, massing, materials selections, etc.) as a function of differences in siting.

A note of caution: The approach to diagramming site data described in the preceding text implies that this part of the design process is orderly, linear, and rational. Some designers consciously work more intuitively. New Mexico practitioner and educator David Vaughan's[18] method epitomizes another approach. He says: "When I do site analysis sketches, I'm almost always plugging-in form; so the analysis and form-making work hand-in-hand on my simple sketches." Figure 2.10 is a graphic snapshot of this characterization of the design process.

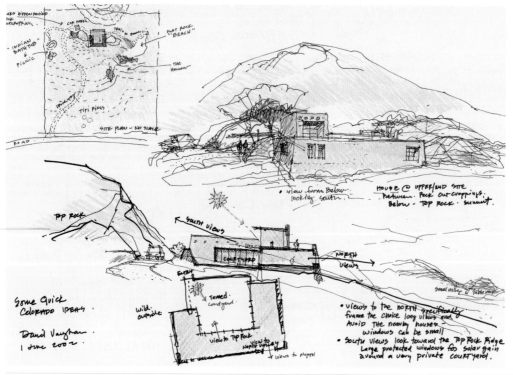

Figure 2.10
Composite diagram including site analysis, architectural concepts, and form possibilities for a private residence in Colorado (© David W. Vaughan).

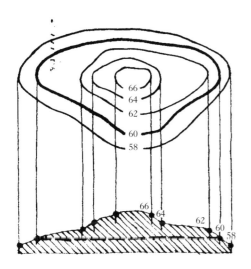

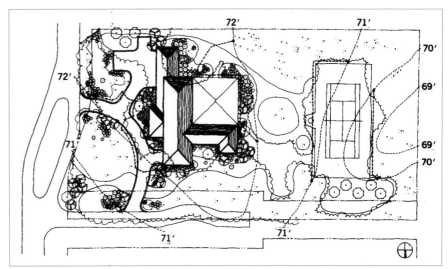

Contour, grading, and drainage: A refresher

A topographic map or "topo" is a detailed and accurate representation of relief or patterns of elevation of the terrain. It also depicts all significant cultural and natural features such as buildings, streams, lakes, and forests. Contour lines on the map trace points of equal elevation or contiguous points of the same altitude. Many clients and a few inexperienced designers find it difficult at first to interpret these maps, but it takes only a little time to comfortably recognize a contour pattern (i.e., valleys, ridges, uniform slopes, etc.) and relate it to actual field conditions. Cultivate the habit of checking the scale relative to the contour interval shown on the site plan or survey; sketching cross-sections through the site is very helpful and revealing in fully understanding landforms. Contour lines do not cross (except at vertical planes); spaced evenly, they signal a constant slope; close together, a steep slope; far apart, a flat or gentle slope. Again, visit the site, and compare it with contours depicted on the site plan so there is no ambiguity about understanding the shape of the land.

Documenting and analyzing a site includes recognition of surface water. Managing surface water is important to the overall health and well being of a site. Therefore, natural drainage patterns (where water comes from, where it goes, and of course what it does on the site itself) should be understood, mapped, and respected. Surface water runoff flows down-slope, perpendicular to the contours, and—hopefully by design—away from your proposed new building (see Figure 2.13).

Figure 2.11 (left)
Graphic depiction of topography and contours in plan, which are then translated to a cross-section (James Snyder and Anthony Catanese, *Introduction to Architecture*, New York: McGraw-Hill, 1979, reproduced with permission of the McGraw-Hill Companies).

Figure 2.12 (right)
Some amount of grading will probably be required around new structures. In a simple example, note how the contours (represented by dotted lines) were manipulated around the tennis court, house, and driveway for a project in Florida.

The art of parking

Like it or not, the automobile is a fact of life, and parking it may not be pretty. View the accommodation of parking (as well as service vehicles and fire trucks) on your site as another design opportunity. Always be on the lookout for any special design tasks such as this, which may seem to be ordinary or adjuncts to the program—they can be turned into real assets that add much to the architectural identity of a project. Consider it part of the challenge to design an unforgettable, or at least pleasant, part of the entry sequence to the building, which is part of the architectural experience.

"Design parking lots not simply as spaces to store vehicles, but also as courtyards, plazas, gardens, art galleries, farmers' markets, and sports courts," asserts Mark Childs,[19] author of *Parking Spaces*. He suggests that parking can become an important strategic feature of urban design, and says that this architectural approach to rethinking the parking lot "is not simply a matter of spending more money to decorate the parking lot, but rather finding uses and designs that add value (i.e., through increased safety, additional rentable area, or improved public acceptance of the development)."

In general, once an area has been identified as reasonable for parking, design goals include: (1) reducing the visual impact, (2) close proximity to building entries (this may be negotiable depending on the project and typical duration of parking), (3) keeping people traffic and car traffic separated, (4) providing universally accessible spaces very close to entries, and (5) simplicity of layout (minimize turns and number of entrances and exits; in small lots, one outlet for both ingress and egress is sufficient). We've all found ourselves at one time or another trapped in some cramped, mazelike parking lot that should have been in a Hitchcock film—so, strive for simplicity. And avoid dead-ends. Reference books such as *Architectural Graphic Standards* describe specific parking layouts, rules of thumb, dimensions, turning radii, angled parking, aisle widths, number of spaces for a given use (usually mandated by city ordinances), and drop-off design criteria. This is a good starting point from which to understand the basic functional and space requirements, but remember that these are strictly formulaic and imply no innovation.

Achieving a balance between packing in as many cars as possible (in terms of space efficiency) and creating a character and quality consistent with the overall design is vital. These are not necessarily mutually exclusive goals. Consider walkway design, orientation of traffic aisles in relation to the building (if pedestrians are indeed utilizing them, you don't want to force people to slalom between rows of parked cars), landscaping, space for plowed snow, and accommodation of service and/or emergency vehicles. Is there a way of breaking down the scale of the lot so that there's not just one big sea of asphalt? Are there logical separations in the program to accomplish this (i.e., staff, public, service)?

Some examples of reducing the unpleasant aesthetic impact of parking lots include designing earth berms around the periphery, lowering the lot level or proposing a terraced scheme (this strategy tends to preserve sight lines to the building and may depend on topography), constructing walls or other screening devices (which may further give unity to, or hide, the site and building), and changing the shape of the lot itself. Choose appropriately durable materials of contrasting texture and color for walkways in the lot— relate these to materials of other pedestrian paths in the area.

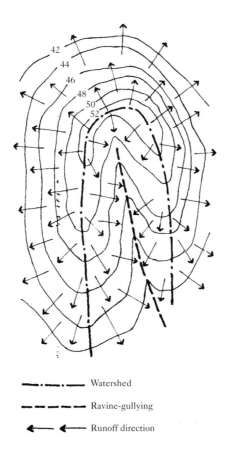

------- · ------- Watershed

---- --- --- -- Ravine-gullying

◄─── · ◄─── Runoff direction

Figure 2.13
Drainage diagram showing
contours in relation to runoff
direction. (James Snyder and
Anthony Catanese, *Introduction to
Architecture*, New York: McGraw-
Hill, 1979, reproduced with
permission of the McGraw-Hill
Companies).

Environmentally sensitive design

The maxim, "First, do no harm," a fundamental principle taught to all medical students, is as pertinent to an architectural intervention with regard to the environment as it is to a medical intervention. Indeed, how can a building be considered beautiful if it damages the environment, compromises the health of its inhabitants, or uses scarce resources?

Designing in resonance with the environment—responding to the forces of nature—has always been a measure of a good design process, exemplified by both the best vernacular architecture and the best architects practicing today. Environmental sensitivity is at the heart of the ethical and social responsibilities of architects.

In order to be effective, environmentally sensitive design must be conceived in terms of an integrated process. Deploying a range of building and site performance strategies (i.e., the building's siting, orientation, massing, fenestration, insulation, shading, natural ventilation and light, materials, etc.) as part of the design process must occur from a project's inception, otherwise it is unlikely they can be effectively incorporated into the project. "There's no question that we need to know the science of how our buildings perform, why they behave badly, and how to make them better. But this is no substitute for great design," says Michael J. Crosbie, Ph.D., AIA.[20] He underscores the point that architects must not only specify the right green widget but consider the full range of design issues—including aesthetics—in other words, a broad and deep integrated design process. It is not sufficient to design merely a green building; the building must also be a work of architecture and all that implies (see definitions of good design, Sidebar 1.1).

There are some incredible new software tools, such as conceptual energy and solar radiation analysis, which can easily guide creative changes to early conceptual design models. For example, modifying the building's shape or orientation, changing materials, or providing shading elements can greatly enhance overall energy performance. The tools can show the architect the energy consequences of design decisions at the click of a mouse. Comparing alternative schemes on the energy dimension are facilitated with such software (see Sidebar 3.3).

In terms of aesthetics, green building strategies may provide opportunities for innovative form-making and articulation. Facts of the site and program may suggest design features. For example, overhangs, light shelves, or other shading devices to control the sun are visible parts of a design that can impart richness and beauty to an elevation while simultaneously solving a problem. Architecture that responds appropriately to varying natural forces, (i.e., solar and wind exposure), will exhibit a purposeful differentiation on each of its elevations. However, the degree to which these architectural responses are treated as expressive elements should ideally be a function of the architectural concept and intention. Moreover, strategies such as selection of a material or component, or a building's orientation on the site do not necessarily suggest a specific style or aesthetic.

La Luz, a community of 96 adobe homes in Albuquerque, New Mexico designed by Antoine Predock, is a great example of architecture that responds to a natural setting. There are spectacular views of the Rio Grande, Sandias, and the downtown from the site, which is on a semi-arid mesa above the west side of the Rio Grande bosque. Predock's basic attitude toward the land: An urban environment and open natural areas can coexist, especially in New Mexico, and the existing natural patterns should be recognized and reinforced. This led to a concentration of development on the high ground of the site. Predock[21] describes how materials and form work together:

> The massive adobe walls serve as heat reservoirs and form acoustical barriers. Some adobe walls are stuccoed white to bounce light into a patio or room. High adobe walls protect outdoor yard areas from wind and provide privacy between units. All exterior walls are earth-colored, stuccoed adobe with sand-blasted concrete lintels spanning openings. Glass is recessed beneath concrete fascias. Glass walls aim east at mountain and city views. The west side units offer a predominately blank wall to the impact of the afternoon sun and are closed to the dust-laden spring winds. The patios offer shelter from winter winds yet act as receptors for trapping solar radiation. Following the existing contours, the units step longitudinally down the hillside.

See Figure 2.14.

Strategies to inform preliminary design thinking
There are a several variations of *A Few Good Architects* (modeled after *A Few Good Men* by Aaron Sorkin, 1992).[22] What follows is one of the better versions of this Tom Cruise-as-Architect/Jack Nicholson-as-Engineer exchange floating around the internet. The parody actually holds some wisdom and underscores the mandate for all of us to fully embrace environmentally sensitive design early in the process, and especially to ensure that engineering consultants are on-board as well.

Engineer: You want answers?

Architect: I think I'm entitled to them.

Engineer: You want answers?!

Architect: I want the truth!

Engineer: You can't handle the truth! Son, we live in a world that has chillers, boilers, and switchgear. And those pieces of equipment have to be located in rooms. Who's gonna design them? You? You, Mr. Architect? I have a greater responsibility than you can possibly fathom. You weep for lost parking spaces and you curse the size of my generator. You have that luxury. You have the luxury of not knowing what I know: that those mechanical/electrical/ plumbing systems, while tragic, probably saved lives. And my existence, while grotesque and incomprehensible to you, saves lives. You don't want the truth because deep down in places you don't talk about at parties you want me on that design team. You need me on that design team. We use words like design, code, analysis. We use these words as the backbone of a life spent providing owner comfort and energy efficiency. You use 'em as a punch line at a party. I have neither the time nor the inclination to explain my design to a man who rises and sleeps under the blanket of the very environment that I provide, then questions the manner in which I provide it! I'd rather you just said "thank you" and went on your way. Otherwise, I suggest you pick up a ductulator and design a building system. Either way, I don't give a damn what you think you're entitled to!

Architect: Did you oversize the mechanical and electrical rooms?

Engineer: (quietly) I did the job you hired me to do.

Architect: Did you oversize the mechanical and electrical rooms?!

Engineer: You're damn right I did!

Figure 2.14
The La Luz community, Albuquerque, New Mexico responds to a spectacular natural setting with building forms, material, and siting (Kirk Gittings Photography).

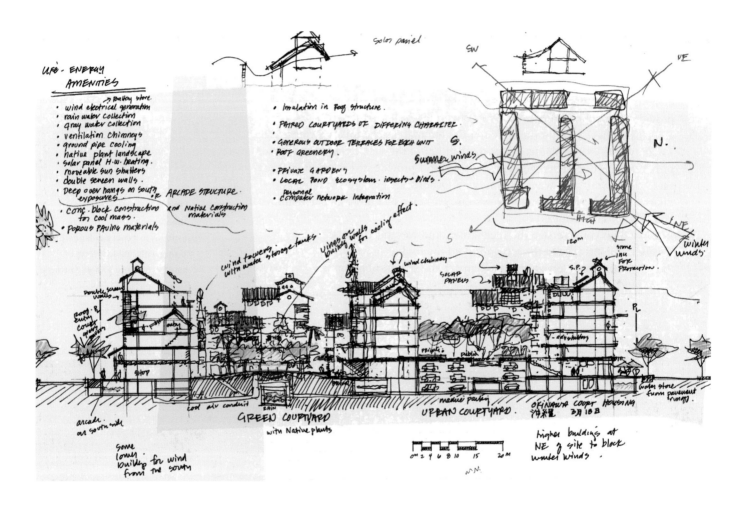

Figure 2.15
Design proposal for courtyard
housing in Okinawa, Japan.
The cross-section reveals
numerous strategies for
environmentally sensitive design
(original drawings by David W.
Vaughan with Nikken Sekkei
Architects, © David W. Vaughan).

Notwithstanding the bias of the engineer portrayed above, it is possible to greatly reduce the size of mechanical rooms and still provide owner comfort. The strategies described in Sidebar 2.2, taking advantage of natural systems for both small- and large-scale buildings, can result in buildings that perform exceptionally well when considered in the preliminary design process.

At this point, basic strategies of green architecture are so well known, says Mike Crosbie,[23] that they can be recited in our sleep. Some of the following strategies may not have a huge impact on form-making but may nonetheless have a huge influence on reducing environmental impact: "Build with local materials, use recycled or recyclable materials,
use diverse energy sources to lessen our dependence on fossil fuels, cut out anything emitting chemicals that deplete the ozone layer, and take advantage of the latest environmental technology." Careful selection and specification of materials, components, and assemblies in conjunction with the strategies set forth in Sidebar 2.2 will yield healthy architecture and advance a healthy environment.

Layers of materials, components, and assemblies typically characterize environmentally sensitive design. Stephen Dent[24] notes:

> Designs will be layered because there are multiple issues to be resolved in responding to and using to maximum advantage the environmental forces of solar radiation, air motion, temperature, humidity, precipitation, and light. No single material or detail can heat and insulate a passive solar building, generate power, collect and recycle water, and provide natural ventilation as needed. Responding to variable forces almost invariably leads to solutions that are not singular and are not fixed.

Therefore, hybrid buildings—those that respond to a unique set of climatic and programmatic conditions with a unique set of strategies—will perform best.

Understanding the microclimate in terms of an architectural response "is knowing how the forces of solar radiation, temperature, humidity, wind, and rain or snow come together on your site," according to Dent. He offers some illuminating examples: "Does the temperature drop during summer nights to a level that is useful for night ventilation cooling? When can a combination of shading and cross-ventilation create thermal comfort in your building? Where is the wind coming from when it is very cold and should be avoided?" The design message is that site-specific climatic forces should be considered in combination—not individually.

Sidebar 2.2: Building performance strategies

Performance strategies for both small- and large-scale buildings, which should be incorporated into preliminary design thinking, are described in this Sidebar by Stephen Dent, a professor at the University of New Mexico and specialist in environmentally sensitive design and building systems.

Smaller scale buildings

The thermal performance of smaller buildings, such as houses or commercial structures under about 5,000 square feet, is usually dominated by the nature of exterior building surfaces. The heating, cooling, and ventilation requirements are largely determined by the orientation and massing of the structure; the amount of insulation; the size, type, and orientation of glazing; shading provisions; amount of thermal storage mass; and potential for natural ventilation. Except in unusual cases, the internal heat gain due to lighting or electrical equipment demands or from occupancy densities is relatively unimportant. These skin load dominated (SLD) buildings are ideal candidates for passive climatic design approaches. After years of research and application in numerous designs throughout the world, we can say unequivocally that this climatic design approach works! With simple design efforts you can economically reduce heating demand by 30 percent in Chicago or 80 percent in Los Angeles. With more aggressive design and construction measures, these levels of performance can be exceeded. It is also easy to greatly reduce cooling demands. Conceptually, the architect should make the building resistant to the negative climatic forces and welcoming to the positive climatic forces. This is where an understanding of the site climate and the thermal requirements of the occupants and the building over time comes into play.

What have we learned about SLD buildings where the dominant energy and comfort concern is with heating?

- *Build well.* Well-insulated buildings with low infiltration levels are a great start. In extreme climates, the use of special framing techniques to allow for thick insulation may be required, and air-to-air heat exchangers are a good idea if infiltration rates are below half an air change per hour. Vapor-permeable infiltration barriers are highly recommended.

- *Collect the sun's warmth.* Orient solar apertures within 30 degrees of south, and try to get solar radiation into all major spaces (while designing shading systems for variable control of direct glare and overheating). You can use 7 to 10 percent of your floor area in south-facing windows if your small building uses light frame construction with no appreciable thermal mass in the construction. (A concrete slab covered with carpet doesn't count!) If the building is frame with significant areas of thermal mass, such as brick floors or masonry partitions, then 13 to 18 percent of floor area in south windows is recommended. And if you build an adobe or masonry home with the insulation on the outside, you may use 20 to 25 percent of the floor area in south glass. These rough guidelines help to prevent serious overheating of the interior on mild days during the heating season. The amount of recommended solar aperture is generally less in warm climates and more in colder climates.

- *Use thermal mass to collect and store the solar heat.* Try to get 5 to 6 square feet of massive materials of no more than 4 inches of thickness for each square foot of south-facing glass. Mass exposed directly to the sunlight is significantly more efficient than that in the shade.

- *Thermal walls and sunspaces.* Thermal storage walls or Trombe walls behind glass areas can provide the necessary collection and storage of solar heat while providing structure and enclosure. Sunspaces such as greenhouses provide for solar collection, usable rooms, and a buffer space between the inside and the harsher exterior environment—besides offering great expressive possibilities for the architecture.

- *Shading.* Know the periods when you *must* have full shading of your windows and when you *may* need shading. The climate is never fully predictable, so there is a strong argument for adjustable or flexible shading systems, which can also be significant architectural elements in the facade. The biggest complaint from owners of passive solar homes is overheating, so don't overdo it. Besides, electricity for cooling is much more expensive than heating fuels.

- *Natural ventilation.* Allow for plenty of cross-ventilation through operable windows, skylights, or vents. If calm periods are a problem in the summer, remember that the ideal situation for inducing ventilation is a low, cool inlet and a high, warm outlet.
- *Glazing.* Use clear double-glazing for maximum solar collection in climates up to 6,000 Heating Degree Days (HDD) and consider triple-glazing or double-glazed windows with night insulation for climates over 6,000 HDD. I recommend low-E windows (with low-emittance coatings) on east, west, or north exposures. For most good-quality windows, low-E glass is now standard or available at low cost. These coatings reflect radiated heat from interior surfaces back into the interior and make double-glazing perform like triple-glazing. This is good news from the viewpoint of building well and for the thermal comfort of anyone near a window on a cold night or hot day.

Larger scale buildings

As buildings get larger, their energy cost problems become dominated by lighting and cooling demands, not by heating. The internal thermal loads caused by the electric lighting, the computers and other electrical equipment, and the occupants themselves often outweigh the thermal loads due to heat gain or loss at the skin of the building. For this reason such buildings are often called internal load dominated (ILD) buildings. Even in cold climates, the areas away from the window walls will need to be cooled all year due to the excess internal loads. When poorly controlled solar radiation is added to the mix, overheating is guaranteed and cooling costs skyrocket. To further complicate the matter, electric utilities typically impose a demand charge on large commercial buildings. This pays for the extra power plant needed to supply electricity for that July afternoon when the temperature is 102°F and employees are at their computers with all the lights on while the copier is humming and the coffee is on! The demand charge can easily double the basic electric bill. There are all sorts of HVAC and control fixes that can help reduce costs in this situation. But doing this for a building that does not respond to its climate can be likened to rearranging the deckchairs on the Titanic—it won't avoid the energy use and financial disaster to come.

However, a building that shades itself from unwanted solar radiation, but is designed in plan and section to admit controlled daylight to replace electric light where possible, can be highly energy efficient, cheap to operate, and a more productive place to work. More and more recent research is leading to the conclusion that employees, not surprisingly, like daylit buildings more than those without access to daylight. But even more importantly for the owners, the employees are more productive in buildings with access to daylight. In a world where technology and productivity are driving the economic engine, this is an important input for designers. (Note that the overall costs of operating a large office building are more than 90 percent in people costs and less than 10 percent in building and operating the facility.)

Following are some rough design guidelines for larger buildings:

- *Think daylighting.* Sunlight is free and should be used wherever possible for the ambient lighting in schools, offices, warehouses, and many other building types. This can reduce electrical lighting usage and costs and, if windows are properly sized, will reduce air-conditioning loads. The designer must be thinking about daylight utilization from the earliest schematics so that such issues as building orientation, massing, sections, and fenestration are coordinated. A thorough understanding of the available sunlight or skylight at your site is needed in order to size openings and design the critical control and distribution components. Daylit buildings tend to have thin sections to maximize the floor area next to exterior windows or atria and higher ceilings to maximize the depth to which the light will penetrate. In general, useful levels of daylight will penetrate into a space a horizontal distance about twice the height of the window head. Light shelves are useful in reducing the illumination intensity next to a window and provide a more even distribution of light in a space. In climates dominated by clear skies, sun control is critical. Your first inclination as a designer will be to use too much glazing. But with the sophisticated glass technology available today and the potential for exterior and interior sun control devices, you can create design responses that are both exciting and effective. In most interiors it is best to bring daylight into a space, but not the direct beam of sunlight—so bounce the light and diffuse it. Due to the computers in many, if not all larger buildings, the designer must reduce brightness levels that are "seen" by the monitor. This, in turn, has led to requirements for lower ambient light levels. Bringing in low levels of glare-free daylight often means the use of tinted glazing and reduced window areas, but more inventive design solutions are possible. More than half of all commercial and school buildings in the U.S. are single storey. Consequently, the openings in the roof surface are ideal for daylighting. It is easier and more natural to distribute light from above, but it will cause overheating if the openings are oversized and there are few control strategies. A great design tool is the daylight model. A replication of the basic room geometry and surface reflectance will yield highly accurate information on daylight levels. In general, with daylight you should bounce it, control it, not overdo it, use it to achieve both ambient light and special effects, and enjoy it!

- *Shading.* This is absolutely critical! You must not allow your designs to overheat because you haven't understood solar geometry and intensity. Besides, responding to the dynamics of the sun's movement can lead to a purposeful differentiation in responses on different building orientations that will bring a unique vitality to your designs. There are a number of exciting design possibilities in new glass coatings, electrically swtiched glass that alters its transparency, double curtain walls with integral shading louvers, and new materials like Cloud Gel which can turn a skylight from clear to translucent at a particular temperature to prevent overheating.

- *Efficient electrical lighting.* Use highly efficient electrical lighting systems that have been designed to be coordinated with the daylighting concept through continuous dimming, step switching, and the use of occupancy sensors. The newest T8 and T5 fluorescent lighting systems with their electronic ballasts offer flicker-free light, good color rendition, and continuous dimming to maintain a constant light level while maximizing the use of daylight—all at greatly reduced power levels. As a matter of fact, complete replacement of an older fluorescent system that uses T12 lamps and magnetic ballasts with the new systems is often paid for in less than three years from the energy cost savings.

- *Natural ventilation.* This is often seen by the mechanical engineer as an obscene phrase, but operable windows and the use of natural ventilation are desirable for the users and can be a major energy-saving feature when properly integrated in the building design.

Daylighting

Use of natural light can be a major form determinant in making architecture and saving energy. Therefore, it should be considered early in the design process and in every subsequent phase including materials and finishes specifications. "Daylight enriches architecture with character," says daylighting consultant Ginger Cartwright,[25] "Changing from morning to afternoon, day to night, and summer to winter,"—and with the weather. Indeed, daylighting is one of the ingredients that makes great architecture magical, imbuing it with a dynamic spirit reflecting the site's unique location, and contributing to the artistic vision. The late Jeff Harner,[26] a Santa Fe architect, commented on the transcendent qualities of light in the southwestern desert: "Here, natural light is almost like a building material." This notion crystallizes the important role that daylighting can play in designing buildings.

Daylight and outside views are precious resources. Every effort must be made to facilitate penetration of natural light and its control (even to below-grade spaces) and promote direct lines of sight to windows for areas inhabited for big blocks of time. Some mechanisms to direct light from outside to inside—other than conventional windows and skylights—include light shelves, sun scoops or light monitors, atria and courtyards, clerestory windows, and finishes that reflect light.

The capture of natural light in a building is an incredible opportunity for sculpting architectural form and also for optimizing energy performance. The resulting luminous environments created within buildings can be delightful and dramatic, particularly in spaces where task lighting is not important to the functions, such as lobbies and circulation areas. Daylighting, or more precisely sunlighting, as lighting designer William Lam[27]

Figure 2.16
A narrow band of Kalwall, a translucent insulated building panel, wraps around the entire roof perimeter of this gymnasium in Princeton, New Jersey (shown under construction), providing enough glare-free natural light to play basketball (Andrew Pressman, FAIA and Siegel Design, Architects).

Figure 2.17
The south-facing light scoop in this house is a soaring architectural feature
above the entry that is not only a sculptural presence on the exterior but brings
sunlight to an interior bridge and stair (photo © Steve Rosenthal).

suggests, is the positive control and utilization of direct light. In harvesting daylight, it is critical to control quantity and quality, including glare, brightness, and distribution, all of which may inform how a building is oriented on its site.

Daylighting is very much rooted in aspects of the site. Climate, latitude, and local weather influence design decisions that align lighting quality and quantity with the specific functions of the building, which have varying lighting needs. In places with clear blue skies, such as in the southwest United States (i.e., the previously cited La Luz), intense sunlight produces deep shadows, strong highlights, and clearly articulated forms. Regions that are characterized by predominately overcast skies, on the other hand, have lower levels of uniform, softer light that does not change significantly as a function of orientation.

When conducting a site analysis with lighting as the focus of the investigation, be sure to consider the impact of adjacent buildings, trees, and ground surfaces on blocking, filtering, and reflecting daylighting. Other local conditions such as pollution may impinge on the character of the light.

Three master manipulators of light and shadow are Alvar Aalto (see Figure 2.18), Tadao Ando, and Louis Kahn. Monographs of their work are filled with extraordinary demonstrations. Kahn once described a building as a "natural lighting fixture." Awe-inspiring words with which to begin preliminary design!

Figure 2.18
Daylight artfully penetrates multiple levels in the Mount Angel library in St. Benedict, Oregon, designed by Alvar Aalto. Splayed surfaces facilitate distribution of daylight within the space (© Lara Swimmer/ESTO).

Precedents and historical perspectives

Why is it useful to know history in relation to designing a building? In a column on an exhibit of the work of McKim, Mead & White, the famed and prolific turn-of-the-century New York architectural firm, Paul Goldberger has written: "These architects looked to history not for something to copy, but for inspiration; to spark creativity."

Analyzing, understanding, interpreting, and finally invoking ideas from the past can facilitate arriving at design solutions in the present and for the future. For example, as Roger Kimball[29] illustrates, Louis Kahn mapped history to contemporary needs. Kahn's design of the Yale Center for British Art is arrayed about "courtyards with commercial rental space on the ground floor, and is reminiscent of traditional Italian Renaissance townhouses." Kimball goes on, however, to proclaim that "nothing could be more contemporary in its use of materials, disposition of light, and ambiance than that elegant urban museum."

"Architects must gain control over the history of architecture—its inevitable influence— and use it," says Lydia Soo,[30] Ph.D., Associate Professor at the Taubman College of Architecture and Urban Planning, University of Michigan. "Knowledge of the history of architecture promotes the kind of broad-mindedness and sensitivity essential to the creation of buildings that end up in history books." Soo suggests that "by understanding past buildings in terms of typological lessons of form, space, light, circulation, structure, material, and so forth, architects can create a repertory of ideas that they can draw from during design. When understood as a lesson in design, the most bygone and dusty building can have immediate relevance." The underlying principles revealed in an analysis of buildings, building components, landscapes, or even communities may indeed have great value in the discovery process of design.

Using precedents in architecture, on the other hand, can be risky. Emerson[31] claimed: "The imitator dooms himself to hopeless mediocrity." If there is no critical thinking, it is all too easy to extract the wrong lessons—for example, strictly visual without rigorous analytic underpinnings. Be wary of accepting prototypes, stereotypes, or fashion out of context. It is essential to analyze form together with as many of the circumstances as possible supporting its development to fully understand the design idea. Then consider how that idea could be tweaked and purposefully applied to assist in creating a new project. *Use the idea, but build on it and make it better.*

At the start of any design project it is useful to become fully informed about similar projects, even those that are considered "cookbook" solutions as a means of quickly ascertaining typical spatial relationships and sizes. This knowledge base can then help to jump-start thinking in creative ways relative to a specific set of conditions. There is no reason to waste valuable design time reinventing the wheel.

In examining precedents, Roger K. Lewis, FAIA,[32] admonishes architects to:

> understand profoundly the nature of the project and all it entails: the client and users, site and context, functional program, building typology, construction and operating budgets, and applicable regulations. Then, in selecting and studying precedents, the designer must decide what is truly relevant.

Lewis suggests that precedents can be categorized by the lessons they impart, which include:

- Function: Similarity in purpose, program, and user population.
- Architectural typology: Traditional building types (e.g., courtyard buildings or row housing) linked to function and form.
- Architectural symbolism: Buildings that deliver messages metaphorically.
- Relation to context: Site, climatic, and other environmental conditions.
- Massing (size and scale) and volumetric geometry.
- Plan and section configuration: Spatial composition and proportions.
- Circulation patterns and modes of movement.
- Interior spatial character: Light, color, texture, ornament.
- Facade composition and character.
- Construction materials, finishes, and details of assembly.
- Structural systems and details.
- Mechanical systems and other environmental control strategies.
- Energy conservation and sustainability.
- Landscape composition.
- Construction cost.

Local and regional traditions

Local and regional building traditions, as manifest in vernacular architecture, can be an incredible source of inspiration to imbue buildings with special content and meaning beyond superficial regional style. Vernacular architecture is typically characterized by a sensitive adaptation to local climate, and "builds on its particular history, cultural values, and natural material resources," says Chris Wilson,[33] Jackson Professor of Cultural Landscape Studies at the University of New Mexico. So, a useful understanding of the vernacular, as a subset of precedent investigations (even independent of building type), can greatly enrich the design process.

A wonderful demonstration of how an architectural design is thoughtfully derived—from a place—is provided by Charles Linn,[34] in an example from *Architectural Record* (April, 2000). Linn critiques the Howard House in Nova Scotia, Canada by architect Brian MacKay-Lyons. The architect's "deep knowledge of the local material culture—an understanding of what materials are used to build, and why and how they are put together" informs the work. MacKay-Lyons creatively employs boat-builders and ironworkers to construct his projects. It is the antithesis of a vernacular pastiche. The house is unconventional—it's not the traditional clapboard frame—but very much appreciated by the neighbors, the fishermen, and the builders, which is a true measure of its success (see Figure 2.20).

Figure 2.19
Precedents (© Roger K. Lewis).

Figure 2.20
The corrugated steel Howard
House, by Brian MacKay-Lyons,
has many of the same features
as the surrounding boathouses
and utility sheds (photo © James
Steeves/Atlantic Stock Images).

Figure 2.21
Jean-Marie Tjibaou Kanak Cultural Center, designed by
Renzo Piano Building Workshop (© ADCK/Renzo Piano Building
Workshop, Architects/Photo John Gollings).

Figure 2.22
Travel sketch of park gazebo
in Sichuan Province, China
(Raymond Novitske, AIA).

Local building traditions can give clues about form, materials, color, and environmentally sensitive approaches to design. In particular, study the orientation, plan organization, and construction details—those commonsense and intelligent strategies that have been proven over time. Classic examples include massive adobe walls for buildings in the southwest specifically designed for a hot, dry climate with cool nights; the closely clustered spaces and compact nature of the saltbox house in cold New England; and the dogtrot house with its open breezeway promoting ventilation in the hot, humid southeast. MacKay-Lyons[35] underscores the message: "The vernacular is what you build when you can't afford to get it wrong environmentally."

As part of precedent investigations and analyses, Chris Wilson makes the case to include local and regional considerations as central to a design practice, which requires a long-term commitment to the study of vernacular traditions. Wilson[36] states: "Delving deeply into the interrelations among architectural form, cultural pattern, local materials, and climate in one region prepares you to more quickly identify pertinent issues in a new setting." The Tjibaou Cultural Center—dedicated to the Kanak culture—in Nouméa, New Caledonia, designed by Renzo Piano Building Workshop, is an excellent example of "paying homage to a culture with its traditions without falling into a parody of it," asserts the Piano firm.[37] Pavilions of varying heights that resemble traditional Kanak huts and clustered in "thematic villages" form the essence of the scheme. Advanced engineering reconciles ancient building customs and traditional materials with steel and glass in a wholly modern expression (see Figure 2.21).

Discovering and researching precedents via books, magazines, the internet, and so on, is certainly valuable and expedient. However, there is no substitute for experiencing places and buildings—both local and distant—first-hand, and that's why travel is an architectural tradition. During recessionary periods when it may not be so easy to find work, traveling is one reliable and fascinating way to keep growing and learning professionally. To maximize understanding and benefit, prepare in advance by collecting plans, photos, and contexts of buildings you anticipate visiting, then study and document the actual environment. Photographs—and of course the traditional travel sketch (see Figure 2.22)—are wonderful ways to record what you see on the road; they are a personal resource that can be treasured and referred to often. And you can bore selected insufferable relatives with a slide show upon your return as an added perk.

Figure 2.23
Window details, Kimbell Museum, Fort Worth, Texas (Edward R. Ford, *The Details of Modern Architecture, Volume 2: 1928 to 1988*, figure 9.39, page 332, © 1996 Massachusetts Institute of Technology, by permission of the MIT Press).

A   Frame from braked stainless steel sheet.
B   Stainless steel splice plate and bolts. The frames are shop-fabricated in panels requiring field splicing.
C   12-guage mill finish (104) stainless steel inner frame epoxied to ½" plywood with glazing bead. The wall's taut appearance is a result of inside glazing.
D   1" insulating glass with stainless steel glazing bead.
E   Stainless steel sill.
F   Stainless steel sleeve to allow inaccuracies between concrete wall and frame to be taken up. Kahn's detail recognized the particular property of each material—the accuracy of the frame and the inaccuracy of the concrete—and chooses these points to emphasize the joints.
G   Notch in concrete column to receive sleeve.

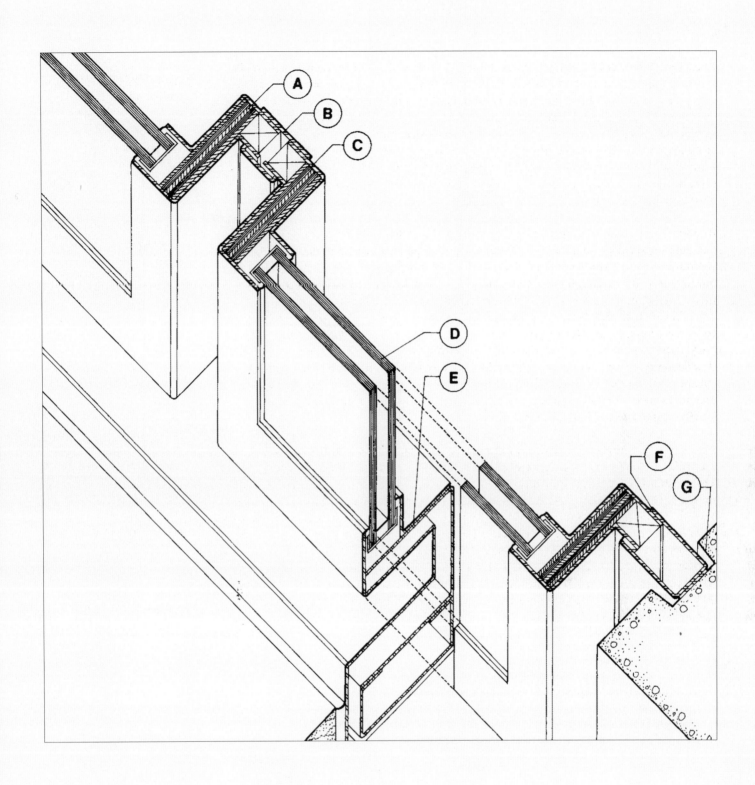

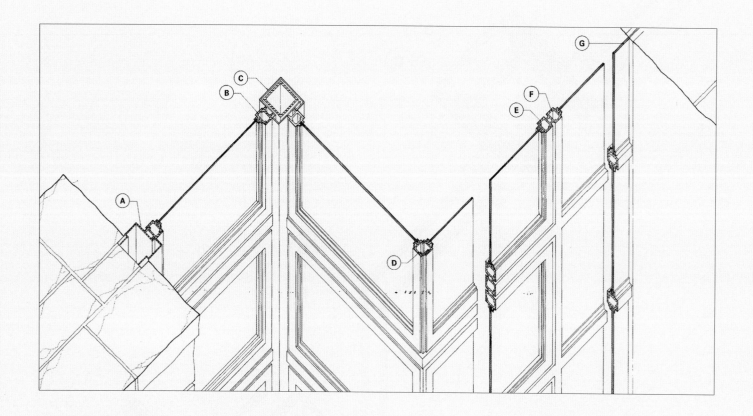

Figure 2.24
Window details in master bedroom, "Fallingwater," Ohiopyle,
Pennsylvania (Edward R. Ford, *The Details of Modern Architecture, Volume 1,*
figure 11.35, page 342, © 1990 Massachusetts Institute of Technology, by
permission of the MIT Press).

A   Jamb of operable sash at stone wall.
B   In-swinging steel casement window.
C   3" x 3" x 3/16" steel tube clad with sheet steel.
D   Corner of out-swinging steel casement windows. There are no meeting
    rails so that the corner is completely free when the windows are open.
E   Operable sash.
F   Fixed sash.
G   Jamb of fixed glass at stone wall. The frame is omitted; the glass is set
    into a notch in the stone with glazing compound.

Construction technology and materials

There is an overarching need in the profession to advance technical design intelligence to create truly great buildings. Work must be infused with both technical acumen and design sensitivity to create buildings that perform exceptionally well and in poetic fashion. To accomplish this, the design process must be focused simultaneously on the big picture and small detail because each will inform development of the other. Shunji Ishida[38] underscores this point in talking about Renzo Piano, with whom he has worked for over 30 years: "From the outset of every project, he keeps in mind the global vision and the nuts and bolts at the same time."

Designing in an office physically removes the architect from the action of construction. Therefore, it is easy for the products of design—drawings and models—to become too much of an abstraction of reality, too much ends in themselves. This is a problem because the architectural design process is meaningless and myopic if it is not truly and completely informed by the construction process. *Always keep in mind what that piece of cardboard or the cross-hatched wall really represents, how it is going to get to the site, who is going to put it in place, and how it will be joined to the adjacent component.*

The art and science of detailing and construction are integral to thinking about architectural design, not only for its realization but also for its impact on form-making, and can be used to strengthen overall design convictions. As with all the other myriad influences impacting design, awareness of the building industry and its standard practices can support design excellence. Knowledge of standard practices is also essential to knowing how best to depart from them in support of an innovative idea. For example, the Aqua, a new apartment and hotel high-rise building in Chicago (designed by Studio Gang), has dramatic and unique curvilinear concrete balconies. The edge condition on each concrete floor slab is different and changes its curves independent of the building's orthogonal core. The steel plate used as the form for the concrete slabs is reset by snapping back into place and then bent into another curve for the subsequent concrete pour. This is a clever idea to reuse the formwork to make a vibrant facade economically feasible.

Construction details
Why should a book on preliminary design be concerned about construction details? Because the best details are a synthesis of science and art; in other words, design is at stake in their creation. Construction detailing should be celebrated as design; the act of detailing can also generate design ideas, and is essential to transforming ideas into a building. Knowledge of how buildings are assembled and detailed is critically important, but often overlooked (and therefore a potentially missed opportunity) in the most important beginning phases of the design process. Indeed, joint details may have a big impact on space planning and floor-to-ceiling heights. In their book *Architectural Detailing*, Edward Allen and Patrick Rand[39] suggest that function, constructability, and aesthetics should be thoughtfully considered when developing details. They give advice on how to design details "that will not leak water or air, will control the flows of heat and water vapor, will adjust to all kinds of movement, will age gracefully, will be easy to construct, and will look great."

The best construction details tie a building to its region and site. Many details that work depend on an appropriate response to local climate and environmental conditions. For example, the position or even use of a vapor retarder in a wall assembly varies between cold and hot, humid climates.

An interesting idea about construction details is that they can play multiple roles. (1) Details, very pragmatically, address connections of components, assemblies, systems, and materials. (2) Architects must consider whether to visually express or conceal those connections, and what the artistic potential in their expression might be. (3) If expressed, the design of details can strongly relate to the larger design concept—or not at all—as a function of architectural intentions.

Here are two wonderful examples of expressing and concealing joints from *The Details of Modern Architecture* by Edward R. Ford. (1) Kimbell Museum by Louis Kahn, Fort Worth, Texas: Window details. "Kahn uses a system of inside glazed, prefabricated frames to eliminate visible joints; the frame corners are welded and ground smooth and the glazing beads are minimal. At the same time other joints are over-expressed—note the space between window frames and the joint between frame and concrete"[40] (see Figure 2.23). (2) Kaufmann House (also known as "Fallingwater") by Frank Lloyd Wright, Ohiopyle, Pennsylvania: Window details in master bedroom. "Wright articulates the bright red horizontal frames and glazing beads while eliminating them at the vertical joint in the stone wall by glazing into a slot in the stone, thus emphasizing the horizontal module of the building as expressed in the 16-inch spaced horizontal bars of the window frames"[41] (see Figure 2.24).

Thoughtfully designed details can imbue a building with character and distinction. Consider this intriguing analogy in the essay, "The Tell-the-Tale Detail" by Marco Frascari.[42] "The architectural details are seen as words composing a sentence. And, as the selection of words and style gives character to the sentence, in a similar way the selection of details and style gives character to a building."

The visual power of detailing can be demonstrated in the simplest elements (i.e., a handrail, a stair, or even a brick wall with raked vertical joints and flush horizontal joints to accentuate the vertical lines). When there is special attention to craft, consistent with that of the schematic building design itself, there is greater likelihood of meaningful aesthetic impact. Indeed, a simple box can be a work of visual art with exquisite detailing and composition. For example, the competition-winning scheme for the proposed new US Embassy in London by KieranTimberlake is a glass cube that has an envelope elegantly designed for sustainability and security. The building envelope consists of blast-resistant glazing and a polymer skin, and solar shading and collection with photovoltaics.

Figure 2.25
Traditional materials tie this house
in southern Maine to its region
(photo © Steve Rosenthal).

The best details can ease the progress of coordination between the various trades involved in building the project. Inevitably, there will be changes during construction, initiated by either contractors or clients. Therefore, in general, some details should be developed with a degree of tolerance so that minor changes will not diminish the vision of the project. In addition, depending on the project, craftsmanship may be an issue—or a break with the traditional ways of building. In this case, details that are bold and designed to withstand less than skillful execution are appropriate (i.e., use of a reveal when changing materials or finishes rather than a flush joint). Selected details, however, will be so important in terms of the tasks performed or by virtue of aesthetic impact that they should not be compromised.

One way to learn about details is to bring a sketchbook whenever you visit interesting buildings. Drawing the details in addition to the larger forms will give you an appreciation for connections. Annotate the sketches with speculations about how the details work and their possible relationship to overarching design goals. Easy retrieval from a sketchbook will facilitate applying the best ideas embedded in your collection to future work.

It is the role of the architect to know where and how to get appropriate information about detailing and how to apply that information to the circumstance, communicate it, and finally, coordinate it with other construction trades. Architect George Heery, FAIA,[43] stated: "The construction technology frontier—where practical, cost-effective construction methodologies are to be found—lies with specialty subcontractors and building-product manufacturers, not with the architect, engineer, or even general contractor." Expertise is found throughout the construction industry; constructors, vendors, fabricators, and industrial manufacturers can contribute significantly to project teams, particularly if they are involved from project inception. Building materials or trade associations, such as the American Concrete Institute, American Institute of Steel Construction, and the American Wood Council, to name a few, provide helpful background information and construction details even if somewhat biased in favor of using the material they represent.

Materials

In terms of the five senses, nothing compares to experiencing materials in the heart of a building under construction (particularly if you've had anything to do with creating the project). For some, even the triumph of the completed work stands as a lesser thrill. The way exposed wood and steel framing, pipes, wiring, ducts, recently cast concrete still in its formwork, wheelbarrow with mortar, and freshly cut lumber—with their respective textures, shapes, voids, and smells—all work together to make architecture is always astonishing.

Selection of materials for a specific application should be considered an important part of the preliminary design process. Certainly there are inherent color, textural, acoustical, fire-resistant, insulative, and other performance qualities across a range of finishes and materials that can support and enrich design concepts (as well as comply with building codes). A material's cost, availability, and its degree of environmental friendliness (i.e., recyclable, renewable), together with its characteristics noted below, all contribute to the decision to specify it.

> "What do you want Brick?" And Brick says to you "I like an Arch."
>
> Louis Kahn[44]

Kahn, in this famous quote, is getting to the heart of what is meant by honesty or essence in the way materials are used in a building. Indeed, it is equally satisfying to observe concrete in compression and steel in tension. In contrast, plastic made to look like stone or stucco that impersonates masonry is an example on the other end of the spectrum.

Understanding a material's unique set of attributes and properties including limitations and visual possibilities—its overall spirit—is essential to material selection, application, and detailing on a specific project. Materials, such as concrete, wood, metals, glass, masonry, and so on, all have properties that can be grouped into the following four categories (as defined by architect Terry Patterson): Form, strength, durability, and workability. Architects can choose to emphasize or subdue these material properties in accordance with the architectural intentions. Patterson[45] asserts: "Understanding the relationship between material properties and their visual impact lets the designer manipulate their contribution to the architectural goals with certainty." Using (and perhaps expressing) a steel cable or rod with turnbuckles for a collar tie in a gable roof is a great example of taking full advantage of the material's tensile strength, and showcasing its elegance by virtue of its minimal profile to resist the outward thrust of rafters.

Patterson[46] cites Frank Lloyd Wright's sensitivity to building materials. "His brick, stone, and concrete block, for example, tended to express the blockiness of masonry in massing and detail. Brick thickness and rectangularity are often emphasized (Robie House pilasters, Morris Gift Shop detailing). Concrete block's mass and rectangularity are often

Figure 2.26
Alternating bands of brick unify seemingly random fenestration on the Arthur M. Sackler Museum at Harvard University (photo © Timothy Hursley).

demonstrated in stepped forms and projecting units (Ennis and other block houses)." Wright occasionally forced a material to do something beyond its physical capabilities to serve aesthetic goals. Patterson explains: "Hidden steel, for example, sometimes helps his masonry and wood achieve remarkable spans that they could never attempt on their own."

Materials can help to connect a project to its site and region. For example, using gray-stained clapboard siding and white trim—traditional materials in New England—on a residence in southern Maine helps the structure to harmonize with its coastal rural surroundings, and succeeds in tying the house's bold forms to the context. The white trim also serves to emphasize the crisp geometry of the three-dimensional forms (see Figure 2.25). Use of readily available, indigenous materials can be economical without the need for energy-intensive and costly shipping and manufacturing (i.e., embodied energy). Local climatic factors should influence material selection to enhance weathering properties and optimize energy conservation. And a local labor pool and craftspeople have the knowledge to work with—easily assemble, maintain, disassemble, and reuse—local materials.

Materials can unify a facade and impart a sense of order. The Arthur M. Sackler Museum at Harvard University by James Stirling Michael Wilford and Associates in association with Perry, Dean, Rogers & Partners demonstrates how alternating bands of gray and brown brick can tie together seemingly random fenestration placement. Different types of windows are centered in each interior space creating the rather disorganized pattern on the facade, which is visually controlled on the exterior by the use of the material (see Figure 2.26).

Consider a materials palette in relation to building typology; research what is typically used and why. High-tech laboratory spaces, gymnasiums, television studios, automobile dealerships, restaurants, hospitals, classrooms, shopping malls, museums, and so on, all have evolving traditions of materials specifications. Understanding that tradition is a starting point for continued evolution and innovation.

Using common materials in uncommon ways can be a great, cost-effective way to innovate. For example, at a most basic level, take a precast concrete "T" (typically used as beams in parking garages) and turn it sideways to form a sculptural parking screen or a bench. Similarly, rotate corrugated sheet metal siding 90 degrees to change its orientation and appearance to create interesting visual contrast, as in the Mead and Penhall residence designed by Bart Prince. And for retail spaces, in which clients are rightly hesitant to spend a lot of money on what is usually leased space, a focus on three-dimensional design rather than on lavish materials and finishes is a great conceptual approach. Sculptural use of such basic elements as gypsum board and metal studs can result in dramatic interior architecture, reinforced by sophisticated use of paint colors.

Materials also include interior finishes. Indoor/outdoor transitions can be controlled—blurred or contrasted—by extending or changing materials from inside to outside. For example, an outdoor terrace that has the same stone finish as the floor of its adjacent living area can make the living area feel more spacious. It is self-evident that more durable and easy-to-maintain materials should be chosen for areas of frequent use (i.e., circulation paths). Also, interiors can be zoned by using similar finishes. Interior finishes can end up inflating construction budgets perhaps more than any other single factor, so consider limiting the use of extravagant and expensive materials to high-visibility public areas.

Materials selection criteria include a range of factors, as a function of project circumstance, as follows:

- alignment with architectural goals and concept;
- cost, initial and life cycle;
- availability;
- relation to context and region;
- response to climate;
- degree of environmental sensitivity;
- ease of construction;
- weathering characteristics and maintenance requirements;
- suitability to the function (i.e., acoustical, fire-resistant, waterproof, insulative, structural, durable, visual, transparent, and so on).

"Lay your hands on materials," suggests Chris Wilson.[47] "A time-honored arts-and-crafts approach to mastering the characteristics and potentials of everyday materials is to build things with your own hands." Wilson suggests ways to do that including volunteering for Habit for Humanity, designing a piece of furniture, or building an addition to your house. Revisiting an old lumberyard or hardware store to see and touch great materials can be an inspiring experience for anyone who hasn't done that in a while.

Budgets

Money and design are inextricably connected. Witness the following two quotes from the classic 1946 book, *Mr. Blandings Builds His Dream House*, by Eric Hodgins.

"There was no way on earth to cut a thirty-one-thousand-dollar house down to a twenty-one-thousand-dollar house any more than there was a way of making marmosets out of a zebra by trimming down and rearranging the zebra."[48]

"'It only costs us the price of an eraser to make our changes now,' [the architect] would say as he obliterated one set of lines to make way for another. 'Get them all out of your system early—they'll cost you real money as soon as the building starts.'"[49]

The project's budget is a major component of the design problem. It is almost always the one big issue for all projects, and includes construction costs, non-construction or "soft" costs, and maintenance and operational costs over the life cycle of the building. Non-construction costs, which usually add about 35 percent to the construction costs, frequently include all professional fees (architect, engineering consultants, attorney, etc.); geotechnical reports; furnishings, fixtures, and equipment; land; building permits; financing costs; insurances; and so on.

A reasonably accurate estimate of probable construction cost can be developed even at the preliminary design phase. This estimate can be based on analyzing the likely components of the initial design scheme given its configuration and a general outline of its materials specifications, plus a generous contingency for the many unknowns (typically 15 to 20 percent). This will yield a project-specific estimate that can be cross-checked against historical gross square-foot costs for a similar building type close to the project's location.

From the first napkin sketches and conversations with the client, it should be apparent that (1) the appropriate stakeholders have agreed to a realistic amount of money required to design and build the project, and (2) any design concept and scheme must be in alignment with that budget mandate. The awareness of funds available for the project is necessary to direct and maximize design possibilities including the building's form, scale, materials, systems, assemblies, and finishes.

In some instances it may be important to clearly set forth the savings of investing in superior materials or systems from the very beginning of a project. In other words, consider the total life cycle costs. Although initial expenses may be higher, savings in reduced maintenance and operating costs—total energy savings—over the life cycle of a building can be significant with this strategy.

Architects should push the limits of the budget in the best interests of the client and project. Architect Will Bruder[50] has stated: "It's not surprising for architects' designs to be over budget since the architect is always striving to achieve the most that is possible for the client." Frequently, innovative designs arise from challenging constraints, including limited construction cost.

Conceptual design cost estimating
Inaccurate budgeting in the conceptual design stage has two major negative consequences, always worth reviewing: (1) If underestimated, schemes will need to be modified, or worse, completely redesigned, resulting in less profit for the architect, less time to complete the work, and perhaps an undermining of confidence in the architect's abilities. (2) If overestimated (or if filled with inflated contingencies to reduce perceived risk), the exaggerated costs could wipe out some potentially exciting design moves.

It is therefore imperative to be cognizant of cost constraints early, and throughout the course of the project, but not to allow the idea of budget limitations to in any way inhibit creativity or innovative ideas. Restrictions in budget may actually improve an architect's work. A large budget implies more freedom of choice, and thus reduced pressure to innovate. Architect Raymond Novitske[51] believes: "Some architects' best work was produced on shoestring budgets because they were forced to be resourceful with what was available or affordable." Novitske bluntly states: "It is fine to think that the high-tech aesthetic came from cerebral designers wanting to strip away the bourgeois, but it is more realistic to believe it was developed by imaginative designers who could not afford finishes."

It is important that clients understand that cost estimating is as much an art as it is a science, particularly for small projects. The laws of supply and demand dominate with regard to prices for materials and labor, which can vary widely by location and over time, particularly with volatile economic swings. And architects are in no position to guarantee a price for work done by someone else; they are making a reasonable professional judgment about expectations of bids by contractors. Architects and their consultants have no control over market forces but they can certainly exercise due diligence in arriving at an estimate of reasonable costs. It is also important to explicitly state what is both included and excluded in the estimate for the construction contract. As previously stated, items such as furniture, fixtures, and equipment and other soft costs are typically excluded.

Another issue related to the art of eliciting a low bid from a qualified contractor has to do with level of detail on design documents. There is a fine line between providing sufficient detail for an accurate cost estimate and over-detailing, which might inflate the cost. Experience and dialogue with the prospective contractors (i.e., having them review and comment on design drawings)—as early as possible in the process—will provide direction.

Seeking professional help—hiring a professional cost consultant during the preliminary design phase—is prudent on complex projects and those located in unfamiliar territory. However, there is, typically, an insufficient fee on small projects to support hiring a cost estimator. So, soliciting cost advice from local contractors (who know the latest materials and prices) can be valuable in the preliminary stages of design with the caveat that objectivity must be maintained throughout the process. If traditional design-bid-build with competitive bidding is envisioned for project delivery, then no advantage can be given to any one contractor providing such advice. When informed by other inputs such as historical data from the architecture firm's own similar projects, a reasonable preliminary estimate of probable construction cost can be developed.

Brian Bowen,[52] an expert in cost management and a retired principal at Hanscomb, Inc., implores us to deal with clients on costing issues, and that one of the most important subjects to broach is contingencies. He says: "Establish from the outset that creation of contingency reserves is a prudent and essential component of good cost control. A good budget should contain adequate reserves to reflect estimating uncertainty at this early stage, to provide for inevitable changes and unforeseen elements, and to cover inflation over the period of implementation." A contingency of 15 to 20 percent of the construction budget is fairly common at the preliminary design phase and is gradually reduced to zero at the end of the construction document phase in proportion to the degree of design resolution.

Communicating cost to a client during preliminary design is as much an art requiring good timing as arriving at the cost. Architect Jeremiah Eck, FAIA,[53] says: "You want the owner's imagination to flow freely in the early stages of the design project, and you don't want to inhibit the client's excitement with constant reminders of what the likely cost might be." At the same time, you must be realistic about the numbers and "engage the owner in the estimating process, making him or her aware early on that price is a big part of design." An objective perspective is key; cost is of great consequence, but so is design quality.

Scope, quality, and cost
Finding the right balance between scope of work, quality, and cost is a crucial part of the design process. The scope of work should be a reflection of programmatic requirements, and quality can be defined by references to built work that the project emulates. Here is an example of a design strategy that balances scope, quality, and cost. The high-visibility public areas of a commercial building—the lobby and primary circulation space—are bathed in natural light, beautiful finishes, and concealed lighting fixtures. In contrast, the more utilitarian areas are treated as loft-like warehouse space with raw finishes and exposed building systems. Both can be beautifully designed and appropriate for function and budget (see Figure 2.27).

Figure 2.27
The highest visibility space in a dermatologist's office is the waiting area. Therefore, design attention and budget was focused here with varied ceiling heights accommodating light coves for indirect ambient illumination, an accent wall of Venetian plaster washed by a recessed perimeter trough light, and a console for a television and display unit (© Christopher Spielmann).

As iterative loops progress in the design process, so too will construction cost estimating. More design information translates to a more detailed construction cost estimate. The new cost information may then suggest a modification to design priorities (or perhaps the budget). Some design strategies might include the following:

- *Efficient space planning.* The less space dedicated to circulation, the more efficient the space plan. The only caveat is that efficiency may need to be balanced with other programmatic and design goals, including aesthetic issues and responses to site conditions.

- *Keep forms simple.* Simple forms, both in three dimensions and in plan, are less expensive to build and require less materials, components, and assemblies, and fewer connections than highly articulated forms.

- *Propose alternate design options.* As early as the schematic design phase, translating some design options into a menu of alternates may be a reasonable tactic to help reconcile budget with cost estimates or actual bids.

Value engineering is a process to determine the systems and materials that will prove most cost-effective over the life, and for the purpose, of the project. Effective value engineering involves a rigorous procedure for optimizing cost, scope, quality, performance, and schedule. Targeting specific areas for potential savings and defining alternative strategies to address those areas without diminishing the spirit of the design are the main objectives. It makes sense, therefore, to be aware of value engineering issues in preliminary design—where the substantive ideas can be appropriately assessed and well integrated into the design—rather than slicing and dicing pieces of the project in later phases. Conducting value engineering during those later phases is where its bad reputation was earned among designers as a cost-cutting, architecture-destroying device.

Consider embracing value engineering in a way that speaks to economy of means in the architectural outcome. The late Charles Moore would always jump at another opportunity to design. Mark Simon[54] has characterized Moore's attitude: "How can we make the project *more* interesting, not *as* interesting when we edit it down?"

Figure 2.28
Pigs with designs for houses of straw, sticks, and brick. Thinking about the right balance between scope of work, quality, and cost should begin early in the design process (© 2003 The New Yorker Collection from cartoonbank.com. All Rights Reserved).

Codes, ordinances, and regulations

There is a full range of codes, ordinances, and regulations that architects must first identify then understand and apply to their specific projects in the local jurisdiction where the project will be constructed. Since they have such a major influence on shaping buildings, familiarity with all the relevant codes related to a specific project must occur at the outset of preliminary design. Codes and their interpretation can be quite complicated and vary between jurisdictions. There may be other community regulations that directly impact architectural design such as homeowners or neighborhood association covenants, subdivision regulations, comprehensive plans, historic district ordinances and historic preservation guidelines, water supply restricted areas, materials and workmanship standards that are referenced in the building code, energy codes, regulations that set forth conditions for tax incentives, and so on. Beware that occasionally some applicable regulations may have conflicting requirements, i.e., a front-yard setback in a covenant is 75 feet and the one in the zoning ordinance is 20 feet. The most restrictive code, ordinance, or regulation is the one that applies to the project.

An egress is a big white bird from northern New England. If you agree with this definition, then spending a bit more time with codes is in your best interest. Even though the prospect of working with codes may be daunting, architect Barry Yatt, FAIA,[55] suggests that they be seen as a resource that "reduces the amount of knowledge you will need for producing workable designs since you can leverage the knowledge and experience embodied in the codes." The architectural design process is, ideally, filled with poetics, magic, and passion but these elements need to be informed by a basic knowledge of the architect's codified responsibilities to the public that ensure the health, safety, and welfare (including minimum livability standards) of building inhabitants. This knowledge must be so ingrained in one's design process that it is like breathing. Codes, ordinances, and regulations have an impact on form-making. Applying them appropriately—capturing the spirit, not just the letter of the law or standard—is essential to realizing design excellence.

Why does design excellence require familiarity with applicable building codes? "Because one can't be cutting-edge without knowing where the edge is," says Barry Yatt.[56] He continues by citing an example: "Without understanding the difference between such building code terms as *project*, *building*, and *fire area*, project teams would likely be forced, through misinterpretation, to design with unnecessarily reduced floor areas. If designers do not understand the differences between fire walls and fire area separations, partitions that might otherwise be opened with windows and railings might remain walled off."

It behooves all of us to embrace codes, ordinances, and regulations as friends and allies in support of great design (and safety), rather than as hurdles to overcome.

Building codes
Building codes have historically evolved in conjunction with responses to disasters in the built environment, such as fires or structural failure. In addition to averting or alleviating catastrophic events, their reason for being has been to establish standards for construction quality that ensure the public's health, safety, and welfare. Therefore, building codes can be considered the construction industry's minimum standard of care.

Building codes, typically produced by national organizations as "model" codes and adopted (in all or part) by local municipalities, determine how buildings are constructed by addressing construction methods and materials related to a building's use, requirements for structural, mechanical (HVAC and plumbing), electrical, water and sewer, and other building systems, components, and assemblies in addition to height and area limitations based on use and construction type. Building codes also address fire protection including emergency egress or exiting, and accessibility.

Examples of model building codes (published before 1994) include the Building Officials and Code Administrators International (BOCA); the International Conference of Building Officials (ICBO), and Southern Building Code Congress International (SBCCI). The successor code to these models, the International Building Code (IBC), was first published in 2000 by the International Code Council, and essentially merges the model codes noted above. New editions of the IBC are promulgated every three years. Local municipalities develop amendments reflecting their unique conditions, and choose when to adopt new editions, so there is some variability across the United States.

There are a number of other specialized technical codes such as the Life Safety Code, the National Electric Code, and so on that are incorporated in whole or part by reference in building codes. To add to the confusion, some states have codes that control design and construction of building types such as hospitals and schools. If there is any doubt about which codes are applicable for a particular jurisdiction, contact the local government to ascertain the code, edition, and related amendments (addressing local conditions) that are in force.

Government agencies issue building permits for projects whose construction documentation complies with their building codes and zoning ordinances. And building inspectors typically track construction as it progresses to verify compliance.

Building codes provide a means of determining the maximum permitted size (i.e., height and area) of the project for its permitted use(s), type of construction and structure, and the fire-resistive requirements of the basic structural elements. There are two items to keep in mind as the preliminary design evolves. (1) Generally, at least two remote means of egress are required (with limits on travel distance to the exit), so, for example, it is customary to locate fire stairs at opposite ends of a structure (see Figure 2.29). In terms of preliminary design, note that expressing exit stairs as vertical elements on the exterior is an example of a code requirement potentially enhancing a building's mass or facade composition. (2) Strive to exceed the minimum accessibility standards for the physically disabled in all the building's primary use areas mandated by building codes and regulations, technical standards, and civil rights legislation such as the Americans with Disabilities Act (see "Inclusive design," below).

Zoning ordinances
Zoning ordinances, produced by local municipalities, direct how land is used (i.e., residential, commercial, mix of residential and commercial, industrial, agricultural, open space, and so on). They are broadly intended to maintain the essential qualities of a neighborhood. Zoning usually regulates height, density, building setbacks (front, side yard, and rear), mass or bulk, area, off-street parking, etc. Zoning also ensures adequate natural light and air movement for building inhabitants.

As with building codes, it is crucial for the architect to analyze the local zoning ordinance at project inception to make certain that the site will accommodate the use and to be aware of all the other constraints impinging on the design. It is frequently helpful to diagram those

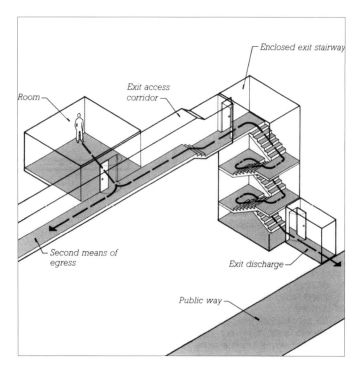

Figure 2.29
The components of an egress system include the exit access, the exit, and the exit discharge (Edward Allen and Joseph Iano, *The Architect's Studio Companion: Technical Guidelines for Preliminary Design*, © 1989 John Wiley & Sons, reprinted by permission of John Wiley & Sons).

constraints and annotate where appropriate to graphically visualize what may or may not be possible in terms of the building's three-dimensional profile.

Euclidean zoning, with its customary separation of land uses that are considered incompatible, is ubiquitous in communities in the United States and is considered conventional. Other types of zoning have been developed in recent years to promote flexibility in mixing land uses, create communities that are more pedestrian-oriented, and develop higher density. Form-based zoning is one such example. Based on principles of new urbanism, form-based codes "address the relationship between building façades and the public realm, the form and mass of buildings in relation to one another, and the scale and types of streets and blocks."[57]

Another type of zoning, incentive zoning, also typically results in increased density (more than would be allowed under the existing ordinance). Developers are given a density bonus or some other benefit such as a faster review process as a reward for providing community amenities such as open space (i.e., park or plaza), public art, improvements or access to infrastructure, or affordable housing.

Inclusive design
Inclusive design, as defined by Karen King and Rebecca Ingram in *Architectural Graphic Standards* (eleventh edition),[58] "is an umbrella that acknowledges the diversity of human beings and in the process embraces a number of positions in relationship to people with disabilities and the built environment. Some positions are mandated and some are advocated (driven by public demand)." Accessible design, for example, is mandated by law under the Americans with Disabilities Act (and many state and local laws, i.e., building codes) and includes minimum standards. This civil rights legislation requires buildings to be accessible and usable for persons with disabilities.

Universal design suggests a different attitude toward design by embodying the spirit of the law that is, that the built environment should be designed for use by anyone including the disabled and able-bodied, small and big, and young and old. It is important to keep in mind that during each person's lifespan, from birth to old age, each of us experiences both the development and loss of abilities (even if the loss is only transitory). Ron Mace,[59] architect and founder of the Center for Universal Design, states that universal design is "the design of products and environments to be usable by all people, to the greatest extent possible, without the need for adaptation or specialized design." The distinction between accessible design and universal design is very important, especially as it relates to the preliminary architectural design process.

Accessible elements are carefully integrated into the overall architectural concept of a universally designed building. Moreover, they do not assume visual prominence as an exclusively accessible feature. Therefore, universal design considerations must be embedded in any preliminary design process. Good designers have always thought about this; generally, accessible buildings are simply better buildings for everyone. For example, finished grade at all entrances meets the threshold to allow anyone access rather than tacking on a ramp to the side of a building's main entrance to accommodate wheelchair users (and to satisfy the letter—not the spirit—of the Americans with Disabilities Act).

Inclusive design—whether codified or not—should be a formative consideration for each project we undertake. Karen King[60] implores us to embrace the human condition—to design for people, all people, not just the "special" ones. She posits:

> When was the last time you thought about the physical mechanics of human beings? How does the human hand work; what does the human gait tell us about the proportion of stairs; how does our physical envelope know hot vs. cold, damp vs. dry, comfort; how do legs work, short, tall, strong, weak, prosthetic, wheels? What changes as we age? The practice of architecture must return to these questions, which are fundamental to why we do what we do.

The imperative for the preliminary design process, therefore, is to imagine how the spaces you conceive will be used and accessed by people across the full spectrum of ages, sizes, abilities, and disabilities, and then to design accordingly.

Notes

1. Herbert Muschamp, "A Philadelphia Show Evokes Kahn's Tough Poetry," *New York Times*, October 27, 1991, p. 34. Muschamp included the Kahn quote regarding Mikveh Israel in the article.
2. Edith Cherry, *Programming for Design*, New York: John Wiley & Sons, 1999, pp. 60–62.
3. Kent Larson discusses design with committees in *Curing the Fountainheadache: How Architects and their Clients Communicate*, Second Edition, New York: Sterling Publishing Co., 2006, pp. 106–9.
4. Edith Cherry, *Programming for Design*, New York: John Wiley & Sons, 1999, p. 58.
5. Steve Martin, *Born Standing Up: A Comic's Life*, New York: Scribner, 2007, p. 192.
6. James Stewart Polshek quoted in "Architectural Ethics" by Suzanne Stephens, *Architecture* vol. 81 no. 3, March 1992, p. 76.
7. James Timberlake quoted in "Accent on Architecture Gala Honors the Best and

Brightest," *AIA Architect*, February 29, 2008.

8. Eliel Saarinen quoted in *Time*, July 2, 1956.

9. Yoshio Taniguchi, interview by Suzannah Lessard, *New York Times Magazine*, April 12, 1998, p. 35.

10. Malcolm Wells, *Gentle Architecture*, New York: McGraw-Hill, 1981, p. 19.

11. Cesar Pelli quoted in "Practicing What He Preaches," by Daralice Boles, *Progressive Architecture* vol. LXX no. 3, March 1989, p. 73.

12. Lewis Mumford wrote the Introduction to *Design with Nature*, by Ian L. McHarg, Garden City, NY: Doubleday, 1969, p. vi.

13. Antoine Predock quoted in "Record Roundtables: The Future of Architecture," *Architectural Record* vol. 179 no. 7, July 1991, p. 177.

14. Fay Jones quoted in "Light and Shadow Only Decoration Park Shelter Needs," by Gareth Fenley, *Architectural Lighting*, March 1988, pp. 25–27.

15. Jean Nouvel quoted in "French Architect Wins Pritzker Prize," by Robin Pogrebin, *New York Times*, March 31, 2008.

16. www.pyatok.com/portfolio/jameslee (accessed on May 17, 2011).

17. John Ormsbee Simonds, *Landcape Architecture: A Manual of Site Planning and Design*, Third Edition, New York: McGraw-Hill, 1998.

18. David Vaughan, personal communication with the author, April 25, 2007.

19. Mark Childs, *Parking Spaces: A Design, Implementation, and Use Manual for Architects, Planners, and Engineers*, New York: McGraw-Hill, 1999.

20. Michael J. Crosbie, "Sustainability: The Duty to Beauty," *AIA Architect*, May 2, 2008.

21. www.predock.com/LaLuz/La%20Luz.html (accessed on May 17, 2011).

22. Thanks to Bryant Rousseau, *Architectural Record* and www.arkitectrue.com/a-few-good-architects/ (accessed on May 17, 2011), July 17, 2007.

23. Michael J. Crosbie, "Sustainability: The Duty to Beauty," *AIA Architect*, May 2, 2008.

24. Stephen Dent, "Environmentally Sensitive Design: A Primer," *Architectural Design Portable Handbook*, New York: McGraw-Hill, 2001, p. 185.

25. Virginia Cartwright, "Shedding (Day) Light on Design," *Architectural Design Portable Handbook*, New York: McGraw-Hill, 2001, p. 222.

26. Jeff Harner quoted in "Firm Profile, Jeff Harner, Architect," by Michael J. Crosbie, *Architecture* vol. 80 No. 8, August 1991, p. 78.

27. William M.C. Lam, *Sunlighting as Formgiver for Architecture*, New York: Van Nostrand Reinhold Company, Inc., 1986.

28. Paul Goldberger, "The City That Was and the City That Is Now," *New York Times*, August 18, 1991, p. 30.

29. Roger Kimball, "Kahn Reconsidered," *Architectural Record* vol. 179 no. 10, October 1991, p. 95.

30. Lydia Soo, "History," *Architecture 101: A Guide to the Design Studio*, New York: John Wiley & Sons, 1993, pp. 78–79.

31. Ralph Waldo Emerson, "Address Before the Senior Class," at Harvard Divinity School, 1838 (see www.harvardsquarelibrary.org/emerson/The-Address.php [accessed on May 17, 2011]).

32. Roger K. Lewis, "Setting Precedents for Using Precedents," *Architectural Design Portable Handbook*, New York: McGraw-Hill, 2001, pp. 58–60.

33. Chris Wilson, "Vernacular Means," *Architectural Design Portable Handbook*, New York: McGraw-Hill, 2001, p. 50.

34. Charles Linn, "Howard House, Nova Scotia, Canada," *Architectural Record* vol. 188 no. 4, April 2000, p. 109.

35. Brian MacKay-Lyons quoted in *The Green House: New Directions in Sustainable Architecture*, New York: Princeton Architectural Press, 2005, p. 116.

36. Chris Wilson, "Vernacular Means," *Architectural Design Portable Handbook*, New York: McGraw-Hill, 2001, p. 51.

37. See the Renzo Piano Building Workshop website, http://rpbw.r.ui-pro.com (accessed on May 17, 2011).

38. Shunji Ishida quoted in "The Incredible Lightness of Being Renzo Piano," by Richard Covington, *Smithsonian*, June 1999, p. 68.

39. Edward Allen and Patrick Rand, *Architectural Detailing: Function-Constructibility-Aesthetics*, Hoboken, NJ: John Wiley & Sons, 2007.

40. Edward R. Ford, *The Details of Modern Architecture Volume 2: 1928 to 1988*, Cambridge, MA: The MIT Press, 1996, pp. 331–32.

41. Edward R. Ford, *The Details of Modern Architecture Volume 1*, Cambridge, MA: The MIT Press, 1990, pp. 341–42.

42. Marco Frascari, "The Tell-the-Tale Detail," *VIA 7: The Building of Architecture*, Cambridge, MA: The MIT Press, 1984, pp. 23–37.

43. George Heery quoted by Nancy B. Solomon, "Design/Build Ventures," *Architecture* vol. 80 no. 9, September 1991, p. 109.

44. Louis Kahn was famous for his proverbs, such as this one quoted in John Lobell, "Kahn and Venturi: An Architecture of Being-in-Context," *Artforum*, February 1978, and Cathleen McGuigan, in "How To Talk to a Brick," *Newsweek*, November 4, 1991.

45. Terry L. Patterson, *Construction Materials for Architects and Designers*, Englewood Cliffs, NJ: Prentice Hall, 1990.

46. Terry L. Patterson, "The Nature of Materials," *Architecture 101: A Guide to the Design Studio*, New York: John Wiley & Sons, 1993, pp. 102–03.

47. Chris Wilson, "Vernacular Means," *Architectural Design Portable Handbook*, New York: McGraw-Hill, 2001, p. 52.

48. Eric Hodgins, *Mr. Blandings Builds His Dream House*, Chicago, IL: Academy Chicago Publishers, 1987, p. 139.

49. Ibid., p. 110.

50. Will Bruder quoted by the author in *Curing the Fountainheadache: How Architects and Their Clients Communicate*, New York: Sterling Publishing Co., 2006, p. 209.

51. Raymond Novitske, personal communication with the author, February 2010.

52. Brian Bowen, personal communication with the author, December 1999.

53. Jeremiah Eck, "Client Relations: Of Timing and Schmoozing," *Professional Practice 101: Business Strategies and Case Studies in Architecture*, Hoboken, NJ: John Wiley & Sons, 2006, p. 145.

54. Mark Simon quoted in "The 2000 Leadership Awards Top Firm," by Vernon Mays, *Residential Architect*, June 2000, p. 50.

55. Barry Yatt, "The Carrot in the Codes," *Architectural Design Portable Handbook*, New York: McGraw-Hill, 2001, p. 138.

56. Barry Yatt, *Cracking the Codes: An Architect's Guide to Building Regulations*, New York: John Wiley & Sons, 1998, pp. 2–3.

57. Form-Based Codes Institute, "Definition of a Form-Based Code," www.formbasedcodes.org/definition.html (accessed on June 16, 2010), February 17, 2009.

58. Karen King and Rebecca Ingram, "Inclusive Design," *Architectural Graphic Standards*, Eleventh Edition, Hoboken, NJ: John Wiley & Sons, 2007, p. 873.

59. Ron Mace, "About UD," The Center for Universal Design, College of Design, North Carolina State University, www.ncsu.edu/www/ncsu/design/sod5/cud/about_ud/about_ud.htm (accessed on May 18, 2011).

60. Karen King, "Meeting the Minimums and Missing the Point," *Professional Practice 101: Business Strategies and Case Studies in Architecture*, Hoboken, NJ: John Wiley & Sons, 2006, p. 368.

Chapter 3
Doing design

Facilitating, promoting, and leveraging all refer to any activity that makes a task easier and perhaps better. Accelerating a solution to a problem, without dictating an outcome, seems to be the essence of process. The topics reviewed in this chapter can be seen as facilitators—or force multipliers. From the results of architectural criticism to the insights derived from modeling, the common outcome is that an energy or creative force is infused into the design process and movement toward goals is promoted. Previously dark corners may be illuminated; alternative perspectives, both literal and figurative, may be suggested; and integration and synthesis ultimately arise more readily from an inventory and analysis of component data (described in Chapter 2).

Rigid methodology may inhibit innovation. Standardized methods for designing, applied across all projects, may be effective in achieving minimal competence (i.e., protecting the safety and welfare of occupants), but they may also limit possibilities. All factors affecting design (programmatic, aesthetic, socio-cultural, site, technical, budgetary, and so on) must be integrated—choreographed—in a mutually reinforcing and case-specific balance. This begins to get at the heart of design process. Therefore, the following material continues to set forth key ingredients—and tools—that are used to strive for excellent design rather than prescribing specific formulae.

Seeking dialogue and criticism

Early in the design process, after you've had a chance to develop design concepts, explore some ideas in-depth, and create a few schemes, expose yourself to as much critical feedback as possible. Peer review and criticism are crucial tools that can elevate the quality of preliminary designs. Basic mechanisms include amplifying or refining ideas, eliminating ideas, and providing new ideas. Cultivate the habit of seeking criticism and engaging in dialogue about the work. Embrace pragmatic and appropriate criticism, be it from clients, peers, or public stakeholders—this represents the kind of criticism that may help projects to be as effective and beautiful as they can be.

Ideally, criticism should strengthen our colleagues and their work, rather than tear them down. Change or adjustment in response to criticism does not have to be seen as compromise, but as something that makes a project more sensitive and responsive to some special issue that may not have been illuminated if not for the additional attention. Another response to criticism is to think of the project as a completely different assignment, which demonstrates that there are many ways to approach a problem. I really hate to admit this, but I almost look forward to criticism because the work usually gets better.

Learning how to wrestle positively with the tough aspects of criticism is central to the ease with which one returns to the critical forum. There are several truisms in this regard. The one most often repeated has to do with avoiding the natural propensity for being defensive. Try to understand precisely what the critic is asserting. If there is any ambiguity, form a hypothesis about what is being said and try to restate the critic's comments. In this way, clarification is more likely (the critic may soften and elaborate in valuable fashion), and you demonstrate your efforts at understanding and correction. But more, dialogue can trigger an idea or line of inquiry not previously imagined that could benefit the work.

All this is not to say that you should always be unconditionally deferential and subservient to criticism from clients, stakeholders, and peers. Part of the value of presenting work to critics lies in preserving your individuality while being responsive to the judgments and suggestions of others. And remember the cliché that criticism is not personal; it's at least supposed to be about the project.

Clients both need and deserve to know substantively why you have made most decisions and why you have ruled out alternative schemes. Not every detail of a project requires justification; you must, however, be prepared to field questions about any detail in order to show why it does not represent arbitrary thinking.

Sidebar 3.1: Tips for doing design

Words themselves can be a powerful tool to facilitate creative thinking and to conceive of innovative space and form. Use words to think about organizing spaces, connecting materials, walking through a building, creating an artful solution. Words that are intentionally vague allow for flexibility in interpretation, thus potentially helping to generate new ideas related to a specific project. For example, what images come to mind when you reflect on words such as node, cluster, screen, layer, modular, interlock, intersect, overlap, reveal, rhythm, focus, procession, and so on? (See also the description of "narrative vision or story" in the section in Chapter 1, "Design attitude.")

Assume that your project will be built. Be confident! This kind of a mindset will create a self-fulfilling prophecy and will at least ensure your personal investment that is so important in designing. Create your own brand of virtual reality: John Simonds in *Landscape Architecture,* Third Edition (McGraw-Hill, 1998) implores us to bring drawings alive—imagine yourself as not just one typical building user, but everyone, from a maintenance person to a manager to a CEO to the public. Imagine how each actor would specifically do his or her job or experience the project. In this fashion, sketches, models, and design acquire life.

Remain flexible and open to new ideas (i.e., sketch constantly and unselfconsciously). Generate as many rough, unconventional, and conventional ideas as possible. Withhold judgment; fight against the natural tendency to erase or delete—use overlays or develop some way to archive the work—you may want to revisit an idea after some design explorations, and see it in a new light.

"Trial, error, and refinement" is an old dictum that constitutes a fine strategy for stimulating creativity. Sometimes, design decisions end up being arbitrary, and you need a starting point from which to jump in. (For the most part, all design decisions should be accountable on some dimension, at least, to facilitate educating the client.) So just put marker on trace and record all ideas. They're always a basis for further exploration, discussion, and evaluation.

Think and design in both two and three dimensions. Moving back and forth between floor plan and model, for example, is a fundamental activity of the design process.

Modify an element in plan, then see what happens in section, physical model, or perspective, and vice versa. That change in plan not only impacts the relationship between immediately adjacent spaces but could have a desirable (or undesirable) consequence for the building's mass, fenestration, or some external expression.

Work in multiple scales simultaneously. This is beneficial for several reasons. It ensures that the big picture is always in mind while not sacrificing attention to detail. Moreover, it may help to keep focus on spatial exploration rather than getting too attached to a single idea (see Figure 3.1).

Embrace failure and criticism as familiar and welcome friends. "Fail often to succeed sooner" is a constructive credo of the innovation and design firm IDEO. Ideas that don't work can provide some of the most useful information and motivation to innovate. View revision as an opportunity to make the work more potent. "Can you learn from mistakes?" is not the question; the question is: "How much can you learn?" There are few temperamental artists who are effective architects.

Seek criticism from other design professionals. Talk to peers; engage in dialogue about general issues and specific project design moves. Find specialists who may offer advice on a particular aspect of a project. See "Seeking dialogue and criticism" on p.96.

Restraint can come at later stages of design. It is not necessary to employ every design feature ever learned simultaneously—but now is the time to try something if the urge is upon you. Edit later.

View specific problems as unique assets. For example, in a renovation there is an existing structural column in the middle of an important space that seemingly disrupts the space. Attempt to highlight it—or make it an integral part of the larger three-dimensional composition; add another (nonstructural) matching column to create a gateway, set up a circulation path, or create a focus or support core.

There are always going to be conflicting priorities; it takes time and experimentation to test possible outcomes for spatial relationships to evolve in accordance with the design concept or theme.

If, however, it appears that too much revision is required, be prepared (and willing) to start anew. The time has not been wasted; the exercise usually results in a deeper knowledge and understanding of the project.

If frozen, work on an unrelated task; come back to the problem at a later time from a different perspective; give ideas a chance to incubate. Isolate the problem; do more research, become more informed about it; return to the site; visit or read about a related and architecturally significant work. Change the medium in which you are working (if hand drawing, build a quick- and dirty physical model or computer model, and vice versa). Alter your routine: Work later or start earlier. Vary your work environment: try a good coffee shop, your dentist's waiting room, or an airport lounge. Some of the best ideas may strike you while taking a shower. Focus on a small idea rather than trying to find the big idea; investigating something of interest may help to jump-start the process and lead to a great concept.

Select the appropriate scale for the design challenge: "Keep the drawings small enough to be drawn quickly and changed easily but large enough to present the needed information" —great advice from Carl Bovill, associate professor at the University of Maryland.

Take small, manageable steps. If at first things seem overwhelming, just chip away one bit at a time. If appropriate, temporarily eliminate minor details so attention can be focused on major elements only. Also view developing a schedule as another design problem— and as a way to define progressive steps. Celebrate meeting the milestones.

Take pleasure in the design process itself and see each step along the way as a satisfying creation in and of itself. Curiosity, playfulness, spontaneity, and a capacity to see—to observe things, people, and behavior in rich detail—are all ways to amplify talent, creativity, and innovative thinking. Going against the grain, embracing the unknown, or looking at life in a manner different than that of the majority can yield fresh perspectives.

Seek economy of means. Strive to wring the most from limited resources. Design ideas that solve multiple problems and at the same time fall into the economy of means category. This notion also has application to meaningful and beautiful form-making in which components are configured and assembled simply to create a rational and artful whole.

Figure 3.1

Here is an example of how a concept for a plan (the geometry of a modified pinwheel) is expressed in a detail (the doors on wall cabinets). Working at multiple scales simultaneously was part of the design process that produced this outcome (© Michael R. Doherty).

Sidebar 3.2: Common mistakes in the design process

Projects are developed where there are lots of terrific ideas and concepts. This can be problematic: When too many things are happening simultaneously, there is no one strong point of view. Do not dilute a good, solid concept with a constellation of clever gestures. *Keep it simple* is the applicable cliché. Albert Einstein said: "Any intelligent fool can make things bigger and more complex. It takes a touch of genius— and a lot of courage—to move in the opposite direction."

Sometimes a designer believes that he or she has such an incredibly good singular idea that it must be carried through, completely intact, to the final scheme. Infatuation should not get in the way of larger goals, and openness to alternatives (perhaps equally infatuating but very different) is the mark of experience. Explore alternatives. Revise. Clients often change their minds midway through a project, or have different design ideas, or simply might not like what you've done for no apparent or logical reason. It behoves you—as the design professional—to be enthusiastic about developing other schemes and responding to new input. Or become a better educator. A great, substantive idea, however, may be worth fighting for.

Avoid the tail wagging the dog syndrome. No one feature should be that precious; do not let an impressive detail dominate decision-making.

Obscure references and concepts that are too personal or that can only be perceived by an elite few are not in the public interest and call into question the role of the professional. But this must be qualified: Sometimes, depending on the circumstances, there may be a good reason for being less than totally self-evident or explicit. One cannot script or predict personal reactions to art—this certainly encompasses the artful aspects of any architectural work. Do make sure that any intentional allusions in the architecture have significant objective impact or meaning. Moreover, ideas must be understood in three-dimensional reality—buildings are not experienced in one-eighth scale, in plan, or in fly-over animations.

Time is one of the most important resources we have. Mismanaging time by working on tasks that do not thoughtfully advance the work is a common occurrence. Constantly monitor what you are doing to ensure that you don't get mired in inconsequential activities.

Some inexperienced designers feel that whatever is drawn must be perfect. This could not be a more inhibiting and destructive belief at the first stages of design. Loosen up! Change can be viewed as compromising design intent. With a different attitude, it can also be viewed as a chance to do more design, and make the project better.

Some if not most designers, not to mention students, feel insecure at some point during the creative process. This is natural: There is always the question of whether you'll come through with the brilliant final product as expected. If you share these feelings, acknowledge and accept that this is the way you operate, and with a systematic approach, perseverance, and experience you will gradually learn that there is really little question about a successful outcome.

Remind yourself that architecture supports or ideally facilitates activity; it is not the end in itself. With a focus on building form rather than the bigger picture of place-making, it is easy to lose sight of this goal.

Clients may ask: "Why did you make that particular design decision?" The value of a thoughtful reason behind important design decisions cannot be over-emphasized, even those involving more subjective issues of taste.

Outdoor spaces that are residual—artifacts of the building mass or articulation—are another common occurrence, and must be avoided.

The art of self-criticism

Self-criticism is an acquired skill, a subset of criticism, that can efficiently stimulate new ideas, infuse projects with special meaning, and help formulate cogent arguments in support of convictions and aspirations. Used properly as a design tool, says Christopher Mead,[1] professor of art history and architecture at the University of New Mexico, self-criticism "serves initially to test the strength of the original idea and then, once the value of that idea has been proven, to ensure its coherent development by editing out missteps or flaws." Every line on the paper or every pixel on the computer screen should relate to the bigger concept, and this is a key issue in critical reflection about a project.

Given that we're all pretty good at design fundamentals—solving the functional equation—it follows that self-criticism ought to be directed at more elusive factors. Mead suggests that this has to do with matters beyond the design's immediate utility; in other words, the question of whether an architect is creating a culturally significant work of art.

Taking an unflinching look at one's own work has tangible benefits. But outside opinions are also helpful. To that end, the notion of peer review, (i.e., discussing work with colleagues), offers an appealing vehicle for the delivery of good criticism.

Peer review

The Boston Society of Architects Works in Progress is a program in which discussing design is the sole intent. Periodically, an architect presents a project in process, and chapter members—and occasionally others from allied disciplines, such as artists, landscape architects, or planners—assemble to constructively critique the work of one of their colleagues. They do it out of the office context and away from the pressures of a business environment. The sessions are intended to provide perceptive discourse to enrich specific projects and advance general knowledge. With the right collection of personalities, this kind of program is a model of professional behavior at a high level, one that in some circumstances could be implemented by even a small group of local design professionals.

The array of constraints may render such programs unrealistic, but the fact remains that it does represent an ideal vehicle for external review. The point is that the more exposure there is to diversity in points of view, the more possibilities become evident. Another great benefit accrues to the reviewer. Experience in evaluating the work of others will likely contribute to more objective and effective ability at self-criticism.

So, in sum, why should criticism be an integral part of the preliminary design process? Christopher Mead[2] believes "criticism applies to every project, regardless of scale or budget: The smallest house addition is as subject to thoughtful analysis as the grandest institutional commission." Moreover, he says: "Criticism can make us see familiar things from new perspectives, shake us out of our shopworn habits, and provoke us into thinking about problems we might otherwise overlook. Criticism, in this sense, is a positive activity …. In questioning a status quo, criticism creates possibilities for change."

Tools: Drawings, physical models, and digital media

As language is central to thinking and communicating verbally, so too are graphic and visual tools central to thinking and communicating three-dimensional form. The overarching message is: Use the tools in the beginning stages of a design project that best augment three-dimensional imagination and abstract thinking. There are no rules; initially, use what's comfortable. It is also important to experiment and develop expertise in a variety of modes.

The following discussion of tools identifies some options for facilitating the design process. Like the process itself, the choice of what to use is quite personal. There are advantages and disadvantages of each tool, and it is often productive to employ a combination of tools at different stages of design, or even simultaneously. The optimal approach is to use what is comfortable, but with an eye toward a tool that complements and works best with the specific task at hand. There are efficiency gains when the products of preliminary design can be built upon and used for construction documents. The caveat is, of course, that the quality of preliminary design should never be compromised for efficiency, and that any tool—hand drawing, software, physical model—may not necessarily be appropriate for every single aspect of the work; if there is a critical message here, this is it!

Do not underestimate the power of serendipity. Creative work is frequently manifest by varying, shifting, and merging contrasting elements. Likewise, varying, shifting, and merging tools and media can spark new perspectives. Moreover, new ideas may become apparent as a function of simply *using* a tool; ideas that were not previously imagined may be discovered, for example, by putting marker to yellow tracing paper, and … playing.

Tools such as napkins and thick markers as well as the ability to deftly move in and out of different software—and between tools and media—will always have a place in the design process. Geoffrey Adams,[3] associate professor at the University of New Mexico, sheds light on this assertion by explaining that there is a fundamental difference between algorithmic computation and associative thinking, which lies at the heart of the human creative act and is the soul of design work. Adams argues that associative thinking, or the ability to bring together disparate information from seemingly unrelated sources to create something new, is easily derailed when the mind is restricted by preconceived notions or seductive but limiting software.

I would offer the notion that "sketching as associative thinking" will always be incorporated into the design process because it is the most immediate brain-to-hand means of expression. Sketching by itself, however, cannot push the design envelope in certain directions as far as evolving software and computing can.

It should be clear, then, that digital and physical methods (i.e., software or freehand drawings and models) are not in opposition. They are simply distinct tools that must be understood in terms of the ways they enhance one's creative thinking at a particular time in the design process. A skillful designer has, at his or her disposal, both digital and physical methods, recognizing that they elicit different dimensions of creativity.

Figure 3.2
This interior perspective of a travel agency is used to both
analyze the appearance of the "floating" ceiling and convey
the feeling of experiencing the space for the client.
The drawing attempts to approximate a photographic view,
although the emphasis is on forms rather than detail.

Figure 3.3
Initial schematic floor plan of the Mottahedeh showroom in
New York. The freehand style is loose and diagrammatic,
suggesting an exploration of possibilities rather than a fully
resolved solution.

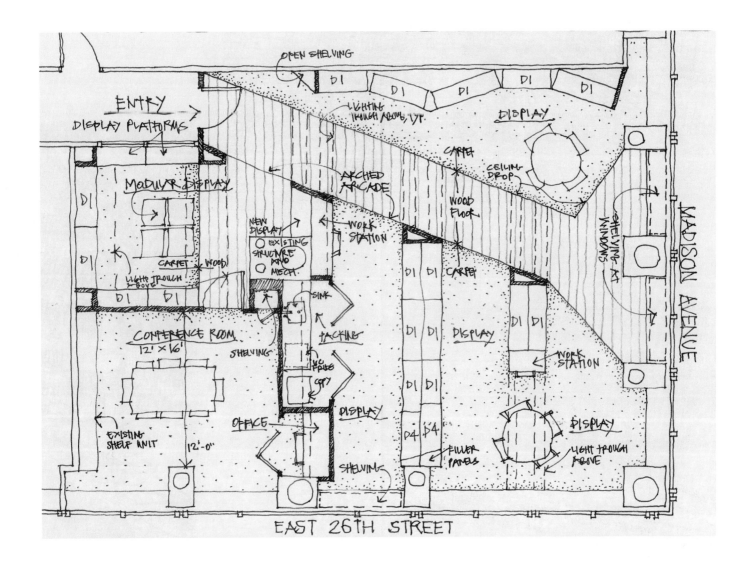

Figure 3.4 and Figure 3.5
First draft (3.4 left) and final
image sketch (3.5 below) used
to illustrate a master planning
services proposal package for a
property in Bangkok, Thailand
(original drawings by David W.
Vaughan with Nikken Sekkei
Architects, © David W. Vaughan).

Figure 3.6
There is nothing like the ambiguous, conceptual, freehand perspective sketch to capture the spirit of a very preliminary design investigation. Shown here is a proposal for a 20,000-square-foot classroom facility in Maine (rendering by Gary Irish Graphics).

Drawings

Just as the smell of sawdust from freshly cut wood at a construction site holds a raw sensual appeal, the feeling of soft pencil, thick marker, or fountain pen on canary trace is almost an end in itself. There should be an inherent pleasure—a mélange of tactile, visual, and auditory stimuli that invite you to continue drawing. The instruments are simple and inexpensive: Pens, markers, pencils, and paper—from sketchbooks to trace—and of course napkins on airplanes (see Figure 4.12(A)), where some of the best ideas are drawn. (One caveat, however, is not to lose sight of the purpose of the drawing, which is to advance the architectural design, not as a work of art in and of itself—even though they often are.)

There is a certain consistency to freehand sketches in early designs—there's an appropriate ambiguity to the lines; things aren't resolved to a high degree conceptually, so why should they be graphically? Hard-line drawings imply a precision that may not be intended by the designer. However, some people find the use of straight edges and hard-lines liberating, and that kind of assertion cannot be disputed. Choice may even be a function of the design concept.

The late Kirby Lockard,[4] in his exceptional book *Drawing as a Means to Architecture*, stated: "Perspective is the most natural way of drawing space, since it is how we see space…. The experience of a building is an infinite number of perspectives." Lockard strongly believed that designs should be studied in perspective, not just in plan, section, and elevation. He goes on to say that the best drawings are never those final presentation masterpieces hanging on the wall, but the ones that showed you the opportunities for improving your ideas, and are now crumpled in the wastebasket. Indeed, a collection of those sketches, shown to a client, could be very compelling evidence for design decisions. They also represent a snapshot of design thinking, which relates to the insightful title of Lockard's book. Drawing enables a "reflective conversation with the situation [you] are shaping," in the immortal words of Donald Schön.[5]

Notwithstanding the efficiency of drawing and modeling on the computer, there are many reasons to practice the art of freehand drawing, and to do it often. First and foremost, drawing the old-fashioned way is a fundamental means for inspiring designs and for personal enlightenment. Cult-like followers of this traditional mainstay of architectural practice will understand. Others should consider this a plea at least to frequently revisit this simple tool. Another point: For many architects, the ability to sketch when visiting a construction site is crucial, especially if a problem arises. Drawing a detail *on the spot* to explain how to join materials, components, or assemblies when there is an unexpected condition, for example, is invaluable in communicating with contractors.

Freehand drawing can also be a powerful and enjoyable means to continue one's education about architecture, which undoubtedly influences design thinking. Architect Jean Pike[6] recalls that Le Corbusier kept a small sketchbook with him and constantly recorded impressions of the physical environment. For Le Corbusier, the drawing was a means to imprint a form or a concept on his memory. The act of drawing allows us to reconnect with the three-dimensionality of the physical world by observing it intimately and over time, and by connecting images with emotion and sensation. Once this intimate knowledge has been recorded in our sketchbooks, revealing what it is that we see and find compelling, we are able to more readily access it and work with it in a way that is truly our own.

Physical models

I'm a great proponent of study models, those that are quick and dirty and can be ripped apart with ease. The best models look like they've been targeted by smart bombs they have so many rips, tears, and changes. Study models used in development of three-dimensional ideas are valuable in many ways, including efficiently presenting multiple schemes to clients. Models are great props for clients who can use them to demystify two-dimensional drawings; they can be touched and are interactive. While three-dimensional digital models serve a similar function, there is a unique element of serendipity that can occur when "playing" with cardboard to manipulate forms, which in turn leads to unimagined results. Indeed, Robert Hull, FAIA,[7] stated in a recent article in *Residential Architect*: "There's something about making physical models, where you don't know where you're going, that makes them essential to design."

Moreover, a physical model is a genuine scaled-down three-dimensional replica of the project existing in real time and space, which facilitates a fairly precise understanding of the building's *entire* form. Patrycja Doniewski,[8] partner of the Philadelphia firm Qb^3, underscores this point in the same article in *Residential Architect*: "We feel the physical 3-D model reveals the truth in scale and proportion and form in a building, and it's easier for us to design in that format because we're not deceived by how something might look in a rendering. It is what it is, not a perspective viewed from somewhere else."

Chipboard, spray adhesive, white glue, scissors; rip it apart, change something, rebuild it—this is one way to construct an effective study model. Chipboard can be cut easily with a mat knife or scissors, and the white glue sets very quickly. Here is a useful technique: (1) Copy preliminary floor plans and elevations. (2) Roughly cut out the copies with scissors. (3) Apply spray adhesive on the back of the copies, and set them on the chipboard. (4) Cut the chipboard following the lines on the copies, and voila, you have the major pieces of the model.

After assembling the parts, or some of the parts—you may want to leave one side open or have the capability to lift off roof or floors to see what's happening inside on larger scale models—experimenting is unbelievably easy. This is where the process becomes fascinating: Use scraps of cardboard to test, develop, and manipulate new forms and sculpt three-dimensional space; cut away part of a floor, and perhaps glue only a small piece of it back. Get some pieces of wood or cut cardboard strips to simulate beams or columns, or build structural components (i.e., trusses). Buy empty plastic bottles from a drugstore in cylindrical or square shapes, and cut them in half to create a vaulted skylight or bay window; do the same with a table tennis ball and you have a small dome—there are many ways to create a rough model kit of parts.

Clockwise from top right:
Figure 3.7
Chipboard massing study of a residence at small scale—1" = 20'. The smaller the scale, the faster to construct with focus on forms, not detail.

Figure 3.8
Study model of chipboard and corrugated cardboard for the interior of a travel agency.

Figure 3.9
Interior study model uses scale people and furniture to help the clients visualize the space and get a sense of scale

Figure 3.10
This massing model was pulled apart and put back together on numerous occasions to investigate design possibilities, and still functioned as an essential part of the client presentation.

Figure 3.11
Quick study models of interior spaces, even though quite crude, can be effective at simulating the impact of daylighting. In this case, the scale was ½" = 1'-0".

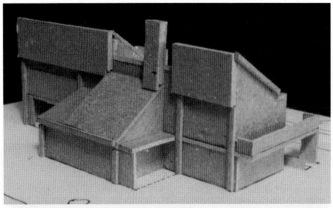

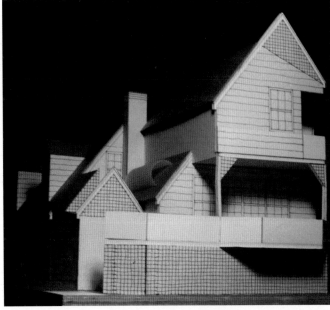

Figure 3.12
Example of a stripped-down study
model (top) used as the basis for
the rendering (bottom), which
helped to communicate the initial
concept of this healthcare facility
to the client.

Return to the floor plan or section, make an adjustment, and see what the implications are in the model (and vice versa). Cut and paste freely—the glue (or tape) makes it simple and quick. Remember to keep the context in mind and build its edges, at the very least, even at the large building scale.

Clay is another effective model material. Its application, though, is usually limited to studying exterior massing in small scale. The material is so plastic that the advantages in molding things are obvious. Children's modular building blocks are also good for the study of massing and give you an excuse to regress in service of the ego.

As an alternative to 3-D modeling software, another added benefit of building a model is that many perspectives can be generated through photography. Photos of study models can be used to block out an infinite number of views, from flybys to worm's-eye, to the most important eye level. Detail can then be added efficiently by drawing rather than building it into the model. Tip 1: Add some scaled grid lines on or in the model prior to photographing; this will help in sketching more accurately. Tip 2: Place the model on a site plan of the same scale; this helps in drawing part of the context (i.e., roads, sidewalks, curbs, etc.).

Digital media

The global familiarity, indeed love affair, with digital media significantly defines the new millennium. The biggest change in architectural practice today is the level of sophistication of the tools. Computing power and software applications are indisputably impressive; they render spectacular simulations of reality and provide other mind-boggling design and documentation capabilities. No technology, however, fully encompasses how a designer thinks. With all the significant innovations and possibilities envisioned with building information modeling (BIM) and other software, there are inherent biases with any modeling tool that may limit utility. Geoffrey Adams[9] underscores this point: "The more complicated and layered a software tool is, the more likely it is to privilege certain methods of working." Adams advises that one always be cognizant of both what the tool is doing *to* the design process as well as what it can do *for* it.

With that caveat, there are incredibly user-friendly programs that are now readily available (i.e., free, downloadable versions) and that can provide new opportunities for design exploration. Google SketchUp, for example, is intuitive, flexible, and has a fast learning curve. Some of its notable features include a push/pull editing tool that extrudes a two-dimensional surface and pushes or pulls it into three dimensions. The shadow engine can help to analyze lighting conditions at any time of the year, any time of day, in any location, including changing the building's orientation on the site. And, as with other modeling programs (i.e., 3D Studio Viz, AutoCad), the ability to get inside the model and look around is a valuable feature as well. Changes are instantaneous with the computer so it is possible to evaluate alternative solutions—including forms, materials, colors, finishes, and so on—as well as to conduct building performance analyses very quickly. Other modeling programs can even test acoustical properties. Activating these capabilities takes full advantage of the power of computing and distinguishes this tool from others such as the pencil. (See Sidebar 3.3 for more information on computational design methods.)

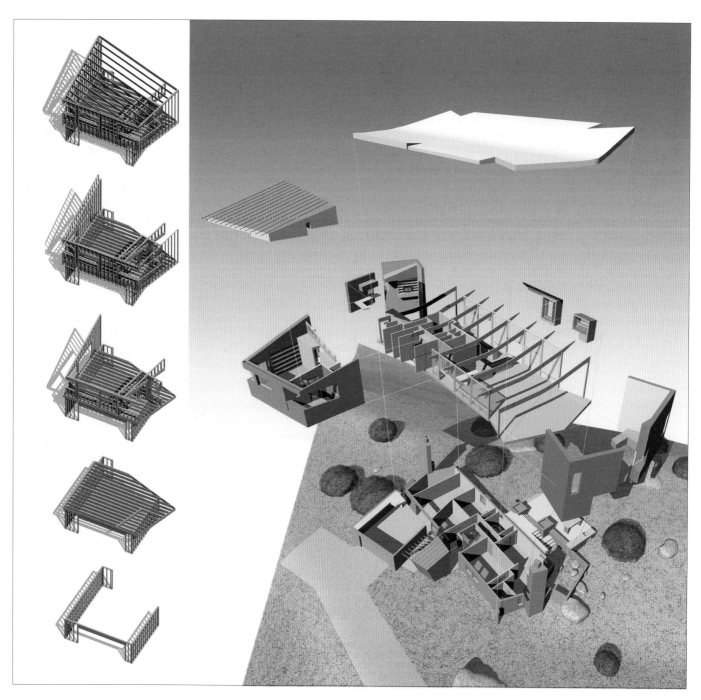

Figure 3.13
(Right) Exploded perspective of a residential project exposes the underlying structural logic of the existing house and reveals a compositional strategy of attaching a series of programmatic components to the whole. (Left) Diagrams explicitly describe the construction of a somewhat complicated double-walled framing system (© Geoffrey Adams).

Phil Bernstein and Joy Stark of Autodesk AEC Solutions wrote this Sidebar to explain how "sustainability easily becomes a natural by-product of design" with sophisticated yet simple-to-use tools. The design process essentially becomes a dialogue with the tool, which helps the architect understand and then optimize the design for energy performance. For more information on building information modeling tools for conceptual energy analysis, go to www.autodesk.com/bim.

Environmental responsibility is no longer an obligation embraced only by altruistic corporations and consumers willing to invest extra time and money for the greater good of the earth. Governments are increasingly mandating environmental accountability, particularly for energy consumption. Since buildings consume disproportionate amounts of energy and produce enormous amounts of greenhouse gas, sustainable design is rapidly shifting from marketing hype to a basic design competency.

Rather than constraining architects, however, sustainability offers new opportunities to expand their influence over the built environment. It adds a new, fundamental dimension that complements aesthetic and functional considerations and becomes a critical criterion by which designs are evaluated. The design process must therefore evolve to incorporate the exploration of environmentally friendly, economically efficient solutions.

Optimizing designs for sustainability has traditionally been a cumbersome process. Design concepts were drawn in 2-D using computer-aided design software from which an analytical model was created to assess building performance. Optimizing project energy efficiency required the tedious exchange of paper drawings between architect and engineer supported by manual calculations, leaving little room for refinement and absorbing considerable fees. If sustainable design is to be adopted by the profession as a practice, barriers to sustainable decision-making must be dramatically lowered.

The ideal moment to optimize a design for energy performance is during conceptualization. Fortunately, design tools have evolved to support the conceptual design process by enabling architects to sketch ideas freely, create forms quickly, and manipulate designs interactively within a 3-D environment (using tools such as Autodesk Revit Architecture software). By starting the design process in a design application such as a building information modeling (BIM) tool, architects gain access to rich data that can help inform sustainability considerations.

While the technology behind such tools is sophisticated, using them should be so simple that sustainability easily becomes a natural by-product of design; this is possible today using commercially available design technology. The process begins with the creation of a simple model with parametric geometry that the architect can use to further develop the design to meet specific project requirements. Working within a software environment specifically designed for conceptual design, the architect starts by drawing the profile of a shape—either a rectangle, a circle, an ellipse, or a curve—which is then translated into a 3-D mass. The mass shape can then be edited through direct manipulation or through establishing specific parameters, such as building height, square footage, and area (see Figure 3.14). Once the shape of the mass is determined, surfaces on the mass can be easily rationalized into various patterns to meet aesthetic, cost, or constructability criteria.

The resulting simple building information model can then be used to derive a conceptual energy model that reports the projected use of energy for the design, based on a preliminary definition of building location, exterior shape, and high-level programmatic information, such as area and volume. The whole-building energy analysis can be computed with the click of a button as opposed to more tedious workflows involving exporting and importing file formats.

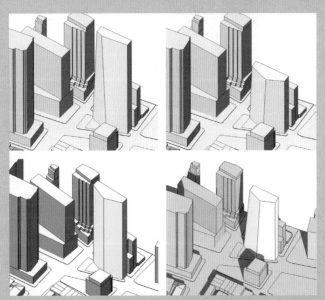

Figure 3.14

Working with a parametric model allows architects to explore design options in accordance with project criteria (courtesy of CASE Design).

With an initial massing and energy model established, the architect is free to explore and refine the design concept by changing the form's geometry, orientation, or enclosure (see Figure 3.15). Any changes made to the conceptual massing model are consistently maintained in the energy model, allowing the designer to compare the energy consumption of all design options explored with total carbon, energy, and water use, and life cycle costs results displayed graphically for easy interpretation (see Figure 3.16).

Solar radiation analysis, which measures the impact of the sun on the building surface, can be derived directly from the conceptual building information model. Designers can use knowledge gained from solar radiation analysis to understand and lower the solar gain for a particular design. They may perform creative steps to alter the building shape or orientation, or may integrate facade details like integrated shading elements to reduce the energy incident on the building enclosure. These strategies can significantly reduce environmental gains and increase overall energy performance for a design (see Figure 3.17). Resulting feedback helps to understand the impact of the sun's shadows based on the specific geographic location of the project site and historic global weather data. As with the conceptual energy analysis, results of the solar radiation analysis are updated immediately when changes are made to the concept model, allowing the designer to easily discover how changes to the design's geometry, orientation, and materials impact the performance.

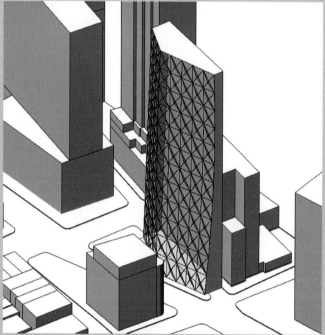

Figure 3.15
(Left) Since the underlying masses are controlled parametrically, the architect can continue to update and refine the design, incorporating real-time feedback and modifications, until a solution that meets the project requirements is reached. (Right) Once the design has been refined based on project criteria, architects can quickly and easily use the parametric mass to generate an analytical model (courtesy of CASE Design).

Using conceptual energy and solar radiation analysis tools, an architect can quickly grasp the implications of early design decisions on long-term sustainable performance of their built projects. Once such insight has become a fluid part of the conceptual design workflow that can be performed with minimal effort, the resulting buildings can be efficiently and effectively designed with the best environmental results.

Figure 3.16
Results of the building performance analysis showing total carbon, energy, and water use and life cycle costs results are displayed graphically to facilitate interpretation and comparison (courtesy of CASE Design).

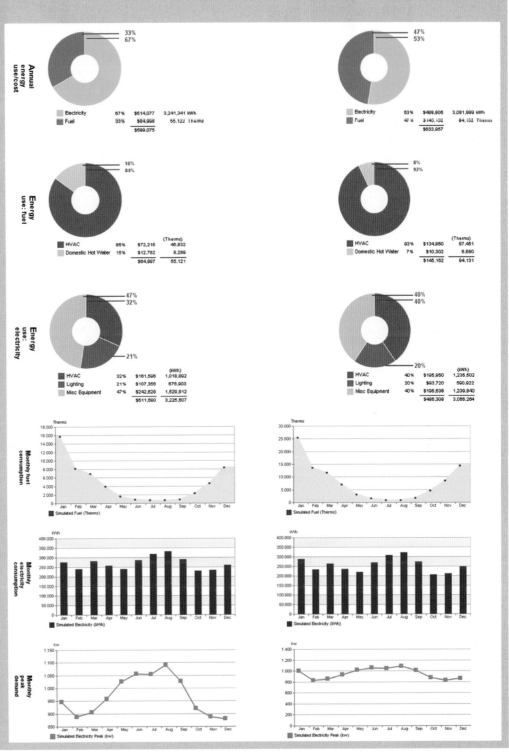

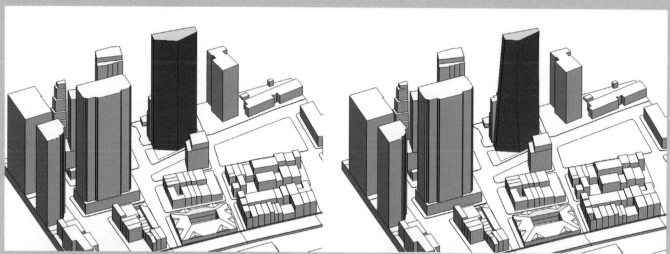

Figure 3.17
Using an interactive solar radiation analysis tool, architects can maximize
the solar collection of building surfaces for energy savings (courtesy of
CASE Design).

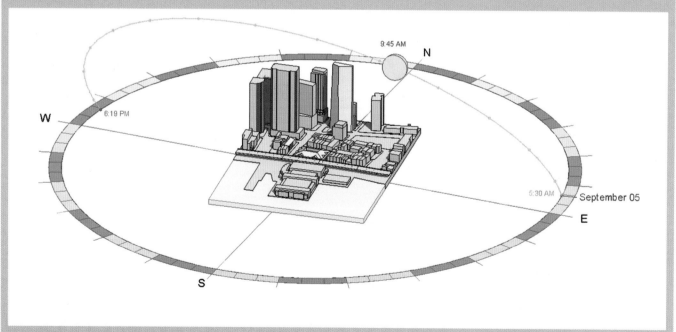

Figure 3.18
Sun path studies can be used to reduce the effects of overshadowing
neighboring buildings, create a more iconic design in context, and verify
that design modifications meet program targets (courtesy of CASE
Design).

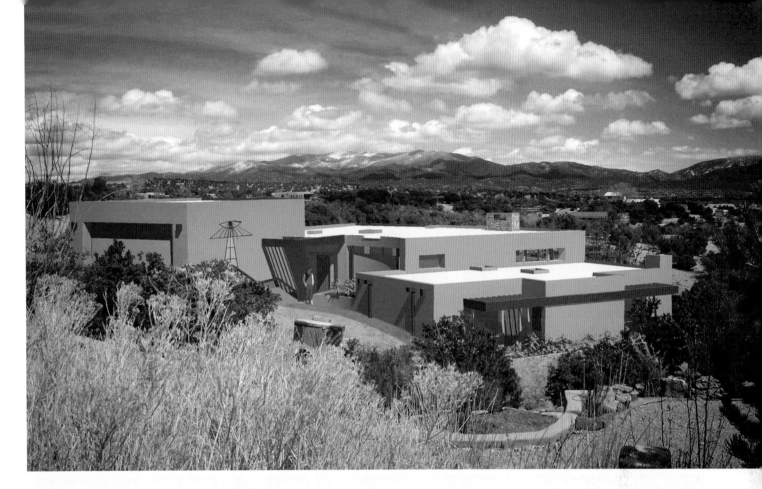

The conceptual design process using BIM software is one of gradual refinement and is analogous to the way an automobile designer sculpts and shapes a large block of clay until the design is revealed. T.J. Meehan,[10] Vice President of CADD Microsystems, describes the conceptual modeling environment in Revit: "Users start with very coarse shapes and continually fine-tune them until the desired amount of detail is created. This process can begin with simple extrusions and evolve into complex, parameter driven, organic shapes."

BIM, of course, is the parametric object-based software that is used to create not only a three-dimensional model of a virtual building, but also 2D drawings and rich databases of information that can include such things as budget estimates, construction schedules, quantities takeoffs, and fabrication details. Parametric modeling allows for substantial changes to be made quickly and for easy interference-checking to occur.

One criticism that has been leveled at computer use at initial phases of design is an inherent focus on precision when there may be a need to be ambiguous. It is possible to view precision as a good thing because specific design moves will work, as schemes evolve to a higher degree of resolution. With loose drawings and study models that is not always the case. Adopting an attitude that embraces digital technology—with a full understanding of its potentials and limitations—enhances the design process.

The great power of the computer and constantly evolving software should be used as a tool to facilitate profound thinking, not simply for the creation of either precisely resolved initial schemes, or at the other extreme, a sea of alternatives. Additionally, it is so easy to neglect the site—and its powerful influences—when focusing on a digital model simply because the context is not usually represented in some way. Taking care to use digital photographs with a three-dimensional modeling program can provide instant context for proposed design schemes. This is an advantageous feature of digital tools because a building model can be superimposed on a site photo and evaluated in context. Whether harmonizing or

Figure 3.19
SketchUp/Photoshop composite image of a house in Santa Fe, New Mexico places the design in its spectacular context and conveys the spirit of the work with great accuracy (Paul Stevenson Oles, FAIA).

Figure 3.20 (top)
Park Café base model shows the architectural facade, establishment of the eye-level perspective, and sun intensity and angle (SketchUp model and tradigital drawing by Jim Leggitt, FAIA).

Figure 3.21 (bottom)
Park Café entourage brings the scene to life with furniture, lighting, signage, steps, stone pavers, plants, trees, and people (SketchUp model and tradigital drawing by Jim Leggitt, FAIA).

Figure 3.22
Park Café final model with all lines, shadows, and materials turned on. Three different tiffs were then exported from the model to be manipulated in Photoshop (SketchUp model and tradigital drawing by Jim Leggitt, FAIA).

Figure 3.23
Park Café modified final model is composed of the three exported tiffs: (1) entire view without any edge linework, (2) pure linework only, and (3) stylized linework with a rough style. The primary view (1) was then altered with a watercolor filter and lightened. That image was then composited with both line drawings, each represented with a 35 percent opacity. The final tiff was plotted on coated bond paper (SketchUp model and tradigital drawing by Jim Leggitt, FAIA).

Figure 3.24
Park Café final color drawing—the large plot was colored with a combination of Chartpak AD markers, Copic markers, and Prismacolor pencils. Much of the image was retraced with a casual line technique. White pencil highlighted certain edges and pencil hatching throughout gave the image character and the much-needed informality of a hand drawing (SketchUp model and tradigital drawing by Jim Leggitt, FAIA).

contrasting with surroundings, design ideas take a position with regard to context and site, and this is one way to evaluate preliminary design schemes in context (see Figure 3.19).

Digital photography is also invaluable for a host of other analytical tasks. Architect Mark Childs, AIA,[11] claims: "the way photographs are used in and around a site gives clues to the nature of the place. What kinds of post cards are in the racks? What images are displayed on buildings and billboards? What do people take pictures of, and where do they stand when doing so?" Sketching over photographs—using them as "foundational drawing surfaces," as Childs says, is another way to get immersed in the site and context.

There is great potential for innovative synthesis in design visualization by mixing-and-matching media. A hybrid image (also known as a tradigital drawing)—a combination of a computer-generated model and traditional hand rendering—can take advantage of the attributes of both modes: The precision and speed of 3-D modeling software with the personal touch and soul of a hand-crafted drawing. Architect and author of *Drawing Shortcuts*, Jim Leggitt, FAIA,[12] is a strong proponent of creating simple SketchUp models, adding entourage to the images using PhotoShop, and finishing the images with hand-drawn textures and color using colored pencils and markers (see Figures 3.20 through 3.24, which show the progression of the image from base model to completed illustration). He claims that this is a great process for architects to experiment and to communicate their ideas.

One great advantage to creating preliminary designs digitally is that the work can be used seamlessly toward the development of orthographic views and construction documents, so there is a process efficiency that is rather elegant. This suggests—together with integrated project delivery (see "Building systems integration and collaboration" later in this chapter)—that the clearly articulated lines between traditional phases of the architectural design process (schematic design, design development, construction documents, and so on) will blur with design decisions being made earlier in the process. The focus on the preliminary/schematic design phase as outlined in this book, therefore, will become even more important in shaping projects, and their ultimate success.

It is interesting to speculate about how the next generation of design tools will facilitate exploring forms and surfaces never before experienced, and therefore advance the design process. Just about anything will be possible and economical, so it is even more important that there be a substantive rationale for design decisions. It is all too easy to be enamored with a "cool" form for its novelty alone. On the other hand, cool forms that relate to a meaningful concept will represent genuine advancement.

Synthesizing program and site issues

Determining how specific program elements and the site fit together is a fascinating exercise. There are analytic questions to consider such as: Do the program and site constantly "fight?" Does one try to change the other to make the relationship work? Is there simply an initial infatuation, or are there long-term implications? Does a mutual support of place and purpose bring out the best qualities in each? Can there be some sort of ongoing dialogue or resonances? In other words, are site and program right for each other?

Figure 3.25
This drawing begins to relate the site data (from Figure 2.9) to program elements—a logical next step in the design process (John Simonds, *Landscape Architecture*, 3rd edn., New York: McGraw-Hill, 1998, reproduced with permission of The McGraw-Hill Companies).

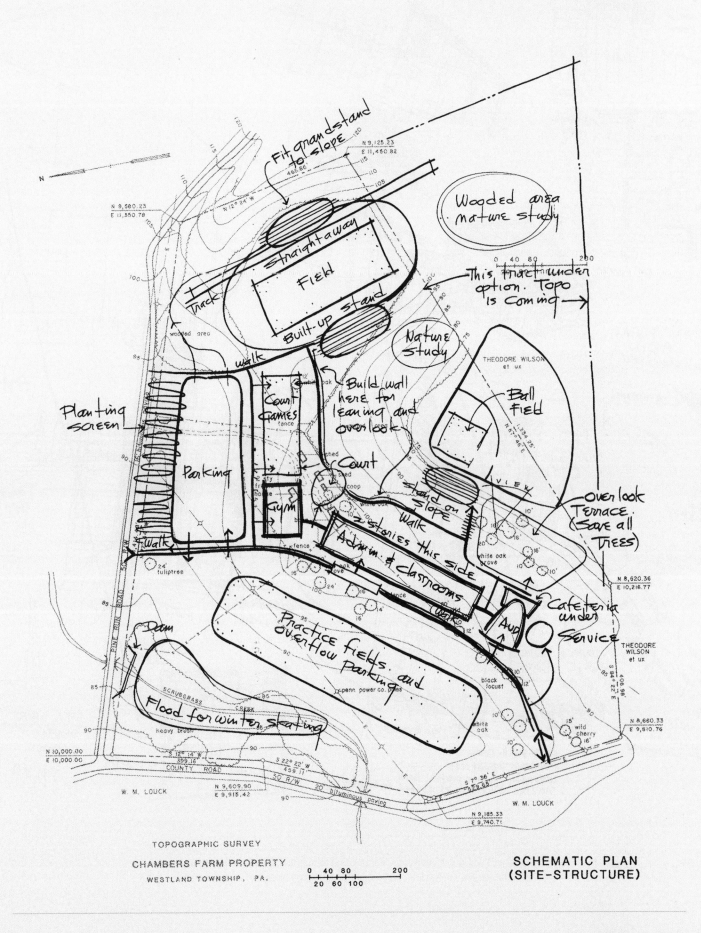

Fit grandstand to slope

Wooded area nature study

This tract under option. Topo is coming

Track

Straightaway

Field

Built-up stand

Nature study

THEODORE WILSON et ux

Ball Field

Planting screen

Court GAMES

Build wall here for leaning and overlook

Court

VIEW

Overlook Terrace (Save all Trees)

Parking

Gym

Stand on slope

Walk

2 stories this side

Admin & classrooms

Cafeteria under Service

Dam

Practice fields and overflow parking

Aud

THEODORE WILSON et ux

Flood for winter skating

penn power co. poles

block locust

white oak

wild cherry

W. M. LOUCK

COUNTY ROAD

bituminous paving

W. M. LOUCK

TOPOGRAPHIC SURVEY

CHAMBERS FARM PROPERTY

WESTLAND TOWNSHIP, PA.

0 40 80   200
   20 60 100

SCHEMATIC PLAN
(SITE-STRUCTURE)

Figure 3.26
Here is a great combination of loose sketches simultaneously examining
spatial and site relationships, and the three-dimensional implications for an
addition to a family cabin in Northern Wyoming (© David W. Vaughan).

Gordon Cullen,[13] in his classic book *The Concise Townscape*, suggests: "There is an *art of relationship* just as there is an art of architecture. Its purpose is to take all the elements that go to create the environment: Buildings, trees, nature, water, traffic, advertisements and so on, and weave them together in such a way that drama is released."

Start testing the goodness of the relationship: The fit of program requirements (perhaps as defined in bubble diagrams) and site potentials (as defined in site analysis diagrams). Begin to arrange the bubbles as an overlay on the site plan (Figure 3.25 is a model for this kind of diagramming). Consider spatial needs together with the physical realities of the site. Also keep in mind the concept for the project. There will no doubt be some conflicts. The design process is becoming more complex and challenging. Remain "cool," block out alternatives and possibilities; this will help to optimize both program and site relationships. Keep these beginning explorations very loose—not too detailed. Make a note to always be aware of, and show the site context in, the medium in which you are working, no matter what the scale. Usually, if it is out of sight, it is out of mind.

Entry sequence
The idea of procession—designing the approach to the site via car (drive-in, drop-off, parking, walking from car to building) or on foot (pedestrian ways from sidewalk to building)—can be a delightful extension of design themes of the building to the larger site context, or a jarring statement about the building and its context. Strive for control over the design of outdoor areas; look for opportunities in the program to charge them with either energy and activity or serenity. This decision can have a lasting impact on the total architectural experience and can contribute to making a distinctive place instead of just a distinctive building.

By itself, the entry sequence can be a rich, eventful experience. It doesn't necessarily have to be the shortest distance between site boundary and entry. There may be an intentionally circuitous path that allows for surprise and discovery. Or, one may catch a glimpse of building to come around one turn, and a panoramic vista may be revealed around another. Such is the experience of traveling to Baxter State Park in north central Maine. After driving about 30 minutes on a seemingly unending monotonous, meandering road surrounded on both sides by walls of pine and birch, the road curves sharply, the woods clear, and the snow-covered peak of Mt. Katahdin looms in the windshield, then suddenly disappears into a new stand of trees. Extraordinary theater.

On the other hand, people who are on a mission, (i.e., walking to work), generally seek the path of least resistance, will cut corners to get there, and become frustrated if there is no direct route. It is important to be aware of the larger design issues in creating a circulation system as a function of project circumstances.

As effective as dramatic punch and soaring emotional response may be, it is salient to reiterate Simonds' notion of harmony—in particular, the importance of harmonizing site elements that form an entry sequence. If the specific design approach engages or grows from the site, the architecture of building entries can be related to the larger site attributes. If the specific design approach is one of drama or contrast (to mutually highlight the best features of both site and building), a more inwardly focused or object-oriented architectural response may be appropriate. Design decisions become less arbitrary when considering the significance of entering the proposed structure in a context beyond the boundaries of the building itself.

Indoor/outdoor transitions

The quality of the relationship of building and site may have a lot to do with how they are physically engaged. Blurring the distinction between these realms can elevate functioning over the entire site. Identify program spaces that would benefit from a flowing of activity or a special dialogue with the outside environment. In many circumstances, design of exterior space is just as important as design of the interior. Therefore, keep in mind how design decisions that define interior spaces can help to simultaneously shape exterior spaces (into outdoor rooms or courtyards, for example). Consider anything that filters or shelters, such as arcades, pergolas, overhangs, and exposed framing. Again, harmony of building design theme and site characteristics helps in form development. Materials can be used to great advantage. Here is a simple example: A lobby opens to a small courtyard; brick pavers used in the lobby extend through the court, serving to unify and reinforce the connection. Moreover, expression of access (physical or visual) to outside space can animate an elevation. For example, Frank Lloyd Wright's Taliesin West in Scottsdale, Arizona is frequently recognized as a building so resonant with its site that the two entities are almost as one. The apparent contradiction lies in Wright's selection of materials and forms, which remain distinct and assertive, yet are perfectly consistent with the desert landscape (see Figure 3.27).

Figure 3.27
Taliesin West, Scottsdale, Arizona designed by Frank Lloyd Wright, resonates with the desert landscape in profound ways (Ezra Stoller © Esto).

Alternatively, indoor/outdoor transition may be defined by a dramatic and abrupt difference between building and site. This approach may serve to focus attention on a particular attribute. Building form and/or materials can support this idea, which in turn should support programmatic goals. For example, Richard Meier's Giovannitti House in Pittsburgh, with its white porcelain enamel panels and bold forms, contrasts sharply with ts suburban setting and appears offset as a unique architectural jewel (see Figure 3.28).

It is worth noting an intention that can be generalized to all projects—particularly at this stage in the design process. The advice comes from noted landscape architect Lawrence Halprin:[14] "Spaces must be designed not only on paper, but also with great emphasis on the sensory experience people will have there—the kinetic feel of movement, the mix of sound and smell, the variety of opportunities for creativity, enjoyment, and human

Figure 3.28
Giovannitti House, Pittsburgh, Pennsylvania designed by Richard Meier, is a unique architectural statement in its suburban context (Ezra Stoller © Esto).

interaction. Constantly remember that the purpose of these designs is to make places for the full range of human experiences."

Organizing elements

Creating order, delight, and a sense of place from large amounts of program and site information, and resolving myriad conflicts is one of the big challenges in preliminary design. The following is a brief review of some typical organizing strategies that will help to address this challenge.

Development of a circulation system—that is, moving from site entry to building and through the building—is a powerful means of ordering and linking the programmed spaces on the site. The program and site analyses will give strong clues about the formal nature of the circulation patterns. For example, a linear scheme may offer interesting possibilities for serial development, clarity, and hierarchy in accessing spaces, and allow for easy future expansion. There are many ways of conceptualizing the linear idea, including the spine, axis, indoor street, arcade, and curved or angled sequential path—all with alternatives and permutations (i.e., parallel, perpendicular, and secondary routes, or even a grid). All of the aforementioned may accommodate a number of special events and contribute quite a bit of variation along the way. Relating functions to the path can establish focal points, or areas of real importance. An axis terminating in a distinctive way can have tremendous impact.

Figure 3.29
Procession is a major aspect of the design of the Mottahedeh showroom in New York City: An angled arcade organizes the space into intimate display zones that change in scale and character as one walks down the axis. Light beams align with columns, accentuating the rhythm of the arcade, and provide indirect ambient illumination (photo © 2005 Norman McGrath).

An example is the stair in the Sainsbury Wing, the addition to London's National Gallery (by Venturi, Scott Brown & Associates). Critic Paul Goldberger[15] describes its function beyond just circulation: "The stair widens as it rises, as if opening up to the art to be found at its top, and as we climb there is a real sense of mounting toward a goal, of aspiring. The stair is not merely a part of the mechanical process of circulation but a potent symbol of pilgrimage toward art." Well-used public circulation areas, including corridors and stairs, can be highlighted as an integral part of a design concept. Figure 3.29, the Mottahedeh showroom, is another example of circulation as essential to the design idea.

Easily perceived circulation is essential to orient the user (especially for very large-scale projects such as hospitals or shopping malls) and to provide information about how the building functions. Ideally, there should be natural cues built into the architecture; a good test is whether lots of signage is required to identify the building from the outside and to know how to proceed on the inside. If all sorts of arrows and directions are necessary, there may be a fundamental problem with the essential form and the order of the building. Also, be judicious in optimizing area and concept: The most efficient buildings are those with the minimum amount of area dedicated to circulation, or those that incorporate segments of circulation into the functional program.

Integration of building systems should be a logical outgrowth and reinforcement of the basic concept and organizing elements. This adds meaning and effectiveness to the architectural concept. Returning to the linear circulation example, the structural system could align on one or both sides of the circulation, and mechanical and electrical systems could have major distribution trunks following the circulation as well. These strategies are potentially very buildable, efficient, and self-evident. Further, as a high-use and high-visibility element, circulation would be an ideal place to focus design attention and budget, a place to revel in the purpose of the project. Use all site factors to full benefit (i.e., daylighting, views); be opportunistic about programming issues (i.e., what functions can spill, mix, or take advantage in some way of this amenity?). The George H. Love '18 Athletic Facility at Phillips Exeter Academy by Kallmann McKinnell & Wood Architects, for example, highlights movement systems as the essence of building organization.

The tradition of utilizing a major central space, the core around which other spaces are organized, is another approach to ordering the program that has stood the test of the ages. When surrounded by functions or circulation on all sides, a central volume becomes an inwardly focused element. Natural light and air can filter into the space, greatly affecting those around it. Examples include atria, lobbies, and courtyards. Nearly every Islamic medieval hospital had a central courtyard with fountains as a primary feature. The air and water were recognized as having therapeutic value in illness, but were also understood as sources of inner comfort, sanctuary, and spirituality. Application of the central space idea along with other forms of circulation is common today. Stunning contemporary examples include the Ford Foundation in New York by Kevin Roche John Dinkeloo & Associates and the James R. Thompson Center in Chicago's loop by Murphy/Jahn (see Figure 3.30).

Other common organizational devices include radial patterns, dispersion schemes (where program elements are separated across a site), doughnut- or racetrack-shaped schemes, and the idea of hierarchy (where most spaces are assigned a hierarchical priority or weight, i.e., convenient location and/or special form for heavy public use, and higher floor and/or more regular pattern for private use). Extending circulation patterns from the larger site context into the building might be an effective way to begin to relate to the surroundings.

Figure 3.30 (right)
The atrium of the James R. Thompson Center in Chicago, by Murphy/Jahn Architects, is an example of how a spectacular central space serves as a focal point for this government building, which contains retail, cultural, and state office functions (Murphy/Jahn Architects).

Figure 3.31 (overleaf)
Piazza San Marco in Venice is a classic illustration of both pleasing proportions of exterior enclosure and buildings designed to work integrally with that exterior space. The angled edges make the outdoor space feel even more expansive.

Clustering or zoning areas of comparable scale and like function may present a most efficient and buildable scheme. At the very least, structural and mechanical system integration will be greatly facilitated. In some instances the fact that massing reflects this special pattern of internal functions and systems may result in an interesting visual manifestation of the program, as in a three-dimensional diagram. This strategy may be used to spur full investigation of three-dimensional potentials. Moreover, the orientation of a "cluster" can be a great environmental strategy. For example, windowless service functions grouped together on the north side can provide a buffer to frequently occupied spaces on the south that might want to optimize solar exposure. Think about the consequences of shadows from a cluster that has a high, large volume.

These may be helpful starting points for initial planning, perhaps to be mixed and matched for efficient functioning and support of architectural concepts. The key is to be in continuous dialogue with program and site data and their analyses to inform dynamic evolution of organizational ideas for the project.

Aesthetic and formal qualities

In architecture school, students are frequently characterized (either by faculty or themselves) as either good at design or good at the technical or engineering aspects of construction. This dichotomy, which places the fine arts and the building sciences at opposite poles, should be shattered because it undermines the mission of creating architecture. Don Hanlon,[16] Professor of Architecture at the University of Wisconsin, Milwaukee, says: "Any knowledgeable and experienced architect knows that beauty and elegance emerge from a complete integration of the poetic and the practical. Aesthetic considerations cannot be divorced from the way something is made or how it functions." The following section highlights design thinking that integrates aesthetic and formal qualities with functional and technical requirements of buildings.

Dynamic three-dimensional sculptural spaces are part of what makes the whole of architecture greater than the sum of its parts. Even the first sketches on napkins should therefore reflect a keen awareness of three-dimensional qualities related to general spatial organization. There is a magnetism, a unique and pleasurable force of attraction produced by buildings that possess volumetric spatial interest. These volumes or spaces may serve as the focus for a project.

In considering the program and site, self-consciously look for opportunities to develop three-dimensional relationships. Examples include lobbies with visual access to mezzanine functions; light scoops for bringing daylight deep into interiors; monumental spaces for special civic impact; and bridges and overlooks traversing great volumes. At the smaller, room scale, the same thinking applies: Should there be differences in ceiling heights (perhaps reinforced by lighting, i.e., lower over workstations for more direct light and intimacy, and higher over circulation for diffuse light and more public scale), or changes in floor height (i.e., raised or sunken levels to help zone activities)? Decisions regarding interior volumes and exterior massing are also likely to give further direction and meaning to the appearance of elevations and perhaps contribute to their composition.

In developing designs, it is important to think in cross-section as well as in plan. Sometimes there is a tendency to get fixated on the plan and extrude the plan diagram in three dimensions. Opportunities might be missed with this diagrammatic focus. It is

worth reiterating the value of amplifying the experience of soaring three-dimensional space. For example, an intentionally constricting, muted corridor leading to an airy open space will generate more emotion and drama than a gradual progression with less contrast. The entry sequence for the Phoenix Central Library, designed by Will Bruder, exhibits such excitement: Ramps from the east- and west-entry doors descend to a central open core, the "crystal canyon."

The idea of enclosure to capture space is relevant. It serves to define an area—both outdoors and indoors, up and down. It can be achieved by a minimum of means, including a simple beam, solid wall, a line of trees, and so on. Kevin Lynch[17] describes the proportions of an external enclosure that people experience as most comfortable: "Its walls are one-half to one-third as high as the width of the space enclosed, while if the ratio falls below one-fourth, the space begins to lack a sense of enclosure." Degrees of openness, flowing space, or tight, confined space are all within control of the designer (see Figure 3.31).

Beauty

> I believe in an 'emotional architecture.' It is very important for human kind that architecture should move by its beauty; if there are many equally valid technical solutions to a problem, the one which offers the user a message of beauty and emotion, that one is architecture.
>
> Luis Barragán[18]

> Architects need to see the building as part of a complex society. But a building is not socially responsible unless it is very beautiful.
>
> James Stewart Polshek[19]

In a discussion of aesthetics, William Strunk and E.B. White,[20] in their famous little primer *The Elements of Style*, describe qualities that can be applied to visual characteristics

Figure 3.32
The School of Architecture and Planning at the University of New Mexico by Antoine Predock Architect in association with Executive Architect Jon Anderson demonstrates how plan and section are connected in a complex relationship linking light, spatial flows, and structure. The building inspires and teaches by revealing structure, environmental systems, and construction details. Materials and forms tie the building to its southwestern context (Paul Stevenson Oles, FAIA).

of buildings: "Here we leave solid ground. Who can confidently say what ignites a certain combination of [forms], causing them to explode in the mind? Who knows why certain notes in music are capable of stirring the listener deeply, though the same notes slightly rearranged are impotent? These are high mysteries." Despite the fact that we know some parts of the brain "light-up" on PET scans when experimental subjects look at certain graphic images, it remains quite impossible to define or predict just what it is that will be embraced as beautiful. What we ought to be aware of are those variables that can be manipulated (see list below) and that may contribute in some reliable fashion to what is experienced as pleasing on some sensual or emotional level.

Much of the aesthetic expression of a building, including massing and basic form-making, materials selection, and elevation development cannot be thought about independently; it may result from a wide range of issues, already integrated into the design process from the program and site analyses. For example, adjacent buildings may have a huge impact in an urban context on specific elevation detailing. A concept related to technological or structural systems may dictate an aesthetic direction; and so on. Usually, basic form has at least something to do with the programmed activity within.

The following is a fairly elementary list of factors (in no particular order) that can be considered, manipulated, and applied in support of design concepts. Note that the circumstances of site and program may call for a specific design feature that has the potential to solve multiple problems simultaneously, which is always a worthy architectural goal. A projecting bay window, as a simple example, might be designed to provide direct sight-lines up and down a street in order to optimize observation of children at play; hence, a potentially dynamic three-dimensional aesthetic feature results from a functional programmatic requirement.

- Scale is an important factor in imagining and designing interior space and exterior massing. It is generally defined as size in relationship to human proportion. Scale can be controlled to reinforce concepts (i.e., grand, to express power or monumentality; small, to encourage intimacy).

  There are various techniques for breaking down the scale of huge spaces that may be dictated by the program. Articulation of building components or materials—even changes in color, for example—can give human scale to a big blank wall. Conversely, over-scaling may be a desirable tactic: Larger-than-ordinary windows for a fire station in a residential neighborhood can serve to reduce perception of overall building size, and thus make the building relate better to adjacent housing.

  A subcategory of may be considered as anthropometrics, or the relationship of human body measurements and performance capabilities to the environments in which specific tasks must be accomplished. This field documents norms or the typical case but becomes crucial when studying how well varied groups or individuals with exceptional characteristics function in a particular space. Young children, the elderly, those who use wheelchairs, or even persons of different ethnic origin may exhibit anthropometric/ergonomic variations that will have an impact on configuration and sizing of architectural elements (see the subsection on "inclusive design" in Chapter 2 on p.90).

- Proportion is an index of the concordance of various parts to each other. Leonardo da Vinci, Vitruvius, and Le Corbusier have devised theories of proportion based on the human form that could be applied to buildings to help create beauty. And there are many other mathematical approaches or geometric systems, including the golden mean and the Fibonacci series. Be sure to consider beauty and harmony of the building components as a part of the greater surroundings.

Alvar Aalto had a contrasting perspective. John Dixon[21] wrote about his work in an editorial in *Progressive Architecture:* "Above all, Aalto demonstrated in all of his buildings design determined by human experience rather than mere abstraction: The changes in ceiling height that signaled degrees of privacy, the windows placed for the view rather than the formal pattern … the handrail shaped for a satisfying grip."

- Light and shadow can be used to articulate or amplify forms (i.e., projecting window jambs on elevations produce shadows, creating a sense of depth and emphasis on verticality).

- Perspective conveys depth and distance. For example, angled walls can seemingly elongate or foreshorten distances (see Figure 3.31).

- Ornament suggests a beautifying accessory that can also be part of an intentionally expressed building system (celebrating the inherent aesthetic of a construction technology), or perhaps some nonfunctional design move (i.e., a stage set to evoke whimsical imagery).

- Focus is a quality that is important in virtually all design disciplines: It crystallizes and draws attention to the most important aspects of a scheme. The focus of a building could be a major public entry, or a main central space—the specific concept will clarify its application and expression. The designer, to reinforce the focus as an important node in the building, might use special massing, scale, materials and texture, lighting, orientation, and so on.

- Visual coherence of all building forms or materials has to do with achieving a sense of harmony. Some unifying thread weaving together disparate parts should be considered. Forms that appear tacked on, almost as an afterthought, or three-dimensionally unresolved, discordant pieces of the program are usually symptoms of too much emphasis on plan.

- The terms symmetry and asymmetry describe arrangements on either side of an axis or center. Symmetry implies a very formal order, whereas asymmetry is less formal and potentially more dynamic. Subtle manipulations in an asymmetrical framework can produce interesting results. For example, the Barcelona Pavilion, designed by Mies van der Rohe, epitomizes the beauty of an asymmetric balance in forms and materials. (The investigation of symmetry/asymmetry from several viewpoints—perception/physiological psychology, cultural anthropology and semiology, and traditional analysis of visual art—can be a fascinating andworthwhile study.)

- Contrast and blending are ideas that have been previously discussed in relation to emphasizing the best characteristics of both the site and the structure. The principles apply at the building scale as well. For example, consider blending in a dense urban site where buildings are tight on either side; the front faces a major street, the back is open to a court. One response might be to pick up the hard edges and solid forms along the street, while the back facade loosens up with softer and more open forms. H.H. Richardson's Glessner House in Chicago exemplifies this strategy, at least in the sense that a fortress-like front facade gives way to an open, almost delicately articulated rear courtyard. In contrast, the entry pyramid at the Louvre in Paris, designed by I.M. Pei, employs the converse strategy with its glazed skin in sharp opposition to surrounding classical forms and textures (see Figure 3.33).

- Rhythm is the cadence of some kind of design theme at a building or detail scale (i.e., fenestration, exposed structure, or material) in some kind of regular pattern or modulation. Varying the pattern of a particular rhythmic scheme may reinforce a concept or highlight a feature. Expanding or contracting the space between recurring elements can add novelty while preserving the rhythmic idea.

- Variety is spice; avoid boring "flavors," arbitrary themes. This is not to say that more neutral or background buildings do not represent good architecture given certain conditions. But even if this type of building is appropriate, there must be something very special about it: Perhaps in its craft, detailing, proportion, or in some aspect that imbues it with the forces of magic and spirit—and beauty.

Color

Ricardo Legorreta[22] describes his fascinating approach to using color in the design process: "I do not say I will make a wall and paint it red. I say I will make something red and it may be a wall."

The world of color and texture is at the architect's disposal, another powerful and potentially inexpensive factor to plug into the design equation, in support of project goals. This can be tied in with a materials selection; certainly the two should not be considered independently. Colors of natural building materials such as wood, masonry, metal, and concrete are limited compared to manufactured colors, which are innumerable. Try not to consider a color scheme only as decoration or something to apply after the design is developed. Color, like any other element, should be part of an integrated approach to the design process. David Childs,[23] commenting on the sometimes subtle yet extraordinary use of color in the Aronoff Center at the University of Cincinnati, designed by Peter Eisenman, said: "I have never seen paint work so hard."

Legorreta[24] reinforces the point by suggesting that color is not simply an adjunct to form-making. Rather, "it is a fundamental element." He continues, in an interview in *Architectural Record*, by stating that color dramatizes form, turns walls into paintings, and stirs emotions. He gathers elements from the building site—rocks, soil, even vegetation—to evoke a feeling in color specific to the location.

Color consultant Deborah Sussman[25] has commented on collaborating with architects: "The architect may want to separate one form from another or to have the envelope read differently from the structure." The sources of her color schemes are quite compelling. Chicago Place on North Michigan Avenue, for example, was based on the "cultural heritage of Chicago," including a "color palette from the works of Louis Sullivan." Sussman[26] summarizes an understanding of color: "Color can evoke memory; it can be a metaphor; it is able to arouse the emotions, stimulating pleasure, comfort, curiosity, confusion, and even anger."

Figure 3.33
A centrally located glass pyramid forms the new main entrance to the Louvre, allows direct access to galleries in each of the museum's three wings, and provides a counterpoint to the surrounding historic building without compromising its integrity (Leonard Jacobson/Pei Cobb Freed & Partners Architects LLP).

Figure 3.34
The color concept for the Santa Monica Village project has two objectives. Below on the base, it creates a light-colored urban frame in formal response to the historic City Hall across the park. Above on the skyline, it provides the townhouse volumes with accent colors to establish a residential scale and a individual identity (Moore Ruble Yudell Architects & Planners and Koning Eizenberg Architecture).

Figure 3.35
Color distinguishes the Santa Monica Civic Center parking garage by Moore Ruble Yudell. A series of bays made of channeled colored glass break down the scale of the structure and are set at varying sizes and angles, which results in light, luminous, and ever-changing qualities (John Linden © 2009).

While keeping in mind specific design objectives for a particular project, such as those noted by Sussman above, there are basic generalizations about color that may be useful—and worth literature review on color theory and design. Some examples include:

- Lighting conditions and sources (i.e., daylight [time of day, location, degree of pollution, cloud cover, etc.], fluorescent, incandescent, low-voltage halogen, and so on) affect how color is perceived.

- Cool colors—greens, blues, violets—tend to recede and make interior space appear larger. Warm colors—reds, oranges, and yellows—tend to advance and make interior space appear smaller.

- Neutral colors are white, black, and gray. A common design strategy that has a big impact is to use a small amount of accent color against a neutral background (see Figure 2.27).

Building systems integration and collaboration

In professional practice, all aspects of a project are part of the design challenge; there is an entire spectrum of design opportunities for the architect to consider, including all the engineering- and technology-intensive building systems. Architects should habitually engage in a design-oriented approach to engineering the building systems. That is, selecting, configuring, and designing details, according to architect and author Edward Allen, FAIA,[27] rather than simply crunching numbers to solve technical problems. On the best projects, architects sustain a focus on the interrelationships between systems, the architectural concept, spatial character, and form.

In the book *Integrated Buildings: The Systems Basis of Architecture*, Leonard Bachman[28] states: "Integration is about bringing all of the building components together in a sympathetic way and emphasizing the synergy of the parts without compromising the integrity of the pieces." He further states that there are three distinct goals of integration, which include physical, visual, and performance, as follows: "components have to share space, their arrangement has to be aesthetically resolved, and at some level, they have to work together or at least not defeat each other." This is a great definition; it is easy to understand why integrated project delivery should be a mandate, if not something to aspire to, on all architectural projects.

Integrating the various building systems and subsystems—typically including structural, heating, ventilating, and air conditioning (HVAC), lighting, electrical, envelope, plumbing, civil, acoustic, vertical transportation, security and fire protection, landscape, interiors, and so on —so that they work together in a coordinated manner must be considered central to the development of preliminary design schemes. *To underscore and reiterate the point: Considering the building systems at this stage of design is the best opportunity to support the architectural concept and organizing strategies, and make them more compelling, buildable, economical, and sustainable.* Moreover, the likelihood of conflicts and complications in later design phases is greatly reduced. Awareness of the technical aspects of the systems, therefore, is a critical element in the creative development of the architecture at this formative stage in the design process.

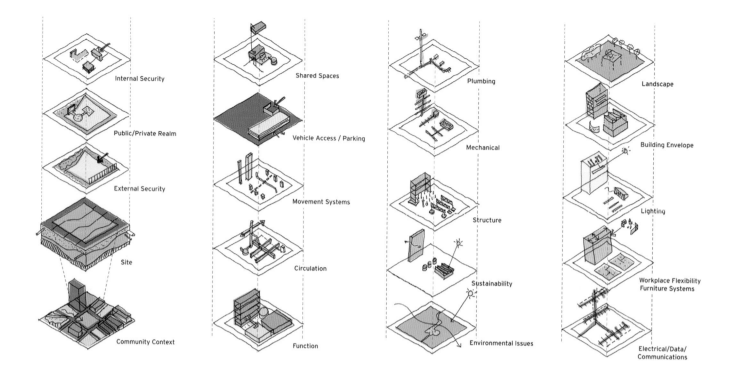

Labels in figure:
Internal Security
Public/Private Realm
External Security
Site
Community Context
Shared Spaces
Vehicle Access / Parking
Movement Systems
Circulation
Function
Plumbing
Mechanical
Structure
Sustainability
Environmental Issues
Landscape
Building Envelope
Lighting
Workplace Flexibility
Furniture Systems
Electrical/Data/
Communications

To lead the design team effectively, the architect must possess a balanced view and have a broad knowledge base (i.e., to select and configure systems) to derive the most from engineering consultants and to make informed decisions about building systems that strengthen design concepts. Integrated project delivery (IPD) is the new term used to characterize the collaborative process in which architects, consultants, and owners work together more closely than ever. IPD is a meaningful response to the marketplace mandate for buildings that are faster to design and construct, at lower cost, as well as more sustainable and of higher quality than those built in the past.

The refrain, "design is a holistic process," cannot be stressed enough. Architect Yann Weymouth[29] summarizes eloquently: "Any architect is trying to make a beautiful building, a wonderful place. To do that you need technology—you need to understand the materials, the structure, the air conditioning, the solar load, the seismic problems. You can't have design without the engineering. It's a whole thing."

Whatever design philosophy is invoked, collaboration, coordination, and understanding of the engineering aspects of architecture are absolutely required by the architect. Individual team members must embrace the idea that caring about project outcomes is far more important than ego. The biggest cultural change in the profession today is not learning how to use new tools and technology, but rather the attitude adjustment required to collaborate effectively with the entire team from the start. Trust, respect, and shared values among team members are essential components of successful collaboration—assuming the highest levels of expertise (see "Collaboration" below).

Figure 3.36
Layers of design that must be thoughtfully considered and integrated early in the process (© 2001 BNIM Architects).

Carl Bovill[30] has developed a cooperative game, the technical integration game, which is one way for the architect and various consultants to motivate creative leaps in designing the building systems in an integrated fashion at the start of the design process. The following is a summary of the game structure.

- Begin the game with the architectural concept and the organization of spaces that support the concept. Developing the basic concept of the architecture is a game in itself that must be played before but also during the technical integration game.

- Over the concept layout of spaces, sketch a solution to each of the technical systems. Annotate the drawings to store information. Do not worry about conflict between systems on this first pass.

- After all the technical systems have been initially laid out, identify and expose the conflict points between systems. Creative inspiration lives on conflict. Learn to follow intuition as well as logic.

- Do not be afraid of intuitive leaps that restructure things. Chance is as important as rules in the creation of form.

- The technical system integration should aid the design concept of the building.

- The heart of a cooperative game is the development of coordinated strategies between the players. Develop strategies of relative importance. In a cooperative game, any player or group of players might become dominant.

- Play the game. Do not settle on the first solution or force system interactions that do not feel right. An old piece of design advice applies here. When the design concept is right, the pieces start falling easily into place.

- Remember that this is a multiplayer game. The designer cannot ignore any of the players. He or she can let some dominate others but cannot ignore some. All the players have to play to reach a solution.

- Remember that play is fun.

Cultivate passion for engineering and construction. The architectural design process is meaningless and myopic if it is not truly and completely informed by construction and engineering processes.

Collaboration
Twenty or 30 years ago, an exclusive focus on becoming a distinctive and uncompromising designer whose solitary brilliance could carry a project might have been embraced and even justified across a profession that celebrated the superstar. Many academic programs still produce students who expect they will spend their careers working as heroic, lone designers. Today, however, while we continue to acknowledge the work of extraordinary designers, it is clearly understood that their role in leading multidisciplinary teams is absolutely essential. Complex programs, the speed with which projects must be completed, high-performance buildings, and a host of economic and political demands require a team of talented and highly trained individuals who are able to collaborate in an effective and efficient manner.

Keep in mind that while the design process involves multiple participants when there is a collaborative effort to develop the architectural design, the tasks or components—as outlined in this book—remain essentially the same. The various analyses, concepts, and other creative impulses serve as points of departure for advancing design schemes, whether arrived at independently or collaboratively. While some design team members may be expert in specific areas, (i.e., structural engineering), or in specific phases in the process (i.e., technical detailing), it is incumbent upon participants to be well versed in all aspects of doing design in order to blur disciplinary boundaries and arrive at a successful integrated design.

While the overarching importance of teamwork has been emphasized (and commercialized) in virtually every setting and pursuit, from athletics to medicine to business, the concept seems packaged more often than not as token effort. Team-building exercises are omnipresent and publicly hailed as valuable, but seem to fall short of anything approaching a serious or an enduring impact. The magic of genuine collaboration seems only to occur among small groups of people who must bond and work together in times of extreme stress. This is a sad commentary. Therefore, it is worth looking somewhat carefully at the essence of collaboration and how it can be achieved within an academic or practice context.

Sustained cooperative and complementary effort among a team of individuals will, at best, maximize adaptability, resourcefulness, readiness, mutual trust and respect, and stress resistance (i.e., fun). A self-proclaimed leadership expert and motivational speaker, John C. Maxwell[31], has developed 17 "indisputable laws of teamwork" in which he attempts to crystallize characteristics of different sorts of teams, and by implication illustrates ways of promoting effective collaboration. A few of the most valuable mandates are as follows:

- The "Law of the Big Picture" and the "Law of the Compass." Team members must be willing to subordinate their roles and personal agendas to support a clear team vision. A team that embraces a vision becomes focused, energized, and confident. It knows where it's headed and why it's going there. A team should really examine its moral, intuitive, historical, directional, strategic, and visionary compasses.

- The "Law of the Niche." All team members have a place where they add the most value. Essentially, when the right team member is in the right place, everyone benefits. To be a good talent scout and put people in their proper roles maximizes efficacy and satisfaction.

- The "Law of the Catalyst." Winning teams have players, (i.e., emerging leaders), often with specific skill sets, who make things happen. These are the catalysts who are naturally intuitive, communicative, passionate people who take the initiative, are responsible, and generous. They are to be nurtured and allowed some autonomy, but not with any hint of favoritism by the designated leader.

- The "Law of Communication." Interaction fuels action. Effective teams have teammates who are constantly talking and listening to each other. This is an extremely important point.

A more prescriptive approach to collaboration is embodied by Team STEPPS,[32] a program of strategies and tools to enhance performance and safety in a clinical environment. This collection of algorithms was developed jointly by the Agency for Healthcare Research and Quality for the Department of Health and Human Services and the Department of Defense, and implemented in virtually all military hospitals. Team protocols comprise four interactive skill areas:

1. **Leadership.** Coordinate activities of the team by ensuring shared goals, adequacy of resources, proper workload, and clarity of overall plan.

2. **Situation monitoring.** Scan and assess situational elements to gain understanding and awareness in support of team function.

3. **Mutual support.** Support team members' needs by understanding responsibilities and workload and empowering alternate viewpoints.

4. **Communication.** Exchange information accurately and readily among team members.

Team process is punctuated by:

- *Planning*—via the "brief," a short session to discuss team roles, expectations, anticipated outcomes, and contingencies.

- *Problem-solving*—via the "huddle," an ad hoc device to reestablish situational awareness and to adjust plan accordingly.

- *Process improvement*—via the "debrief," a review of team performance "after action," toward identifying areas for improvement and recognizing successes.

The inherent theme, then, is that collaboration is powerful and positive, but actually quite difficult to achieve in routine practice with all its realities and influences. Algorithmic prescriptions and sound-bite admonitions help to some extent but really do not do justice to the importance and challenge of facilitating team solutions in the specific context of professional architecture.

Collaboration skills—in conjunction with architectural design skills—are increasingly critical to the successful completion of building projects. They should not slip from our focus. Future education, training, and practice will reflect the increasing requirement for joint coordination among all key participants in the building design enterprise. To paraphrase anthropologist Margaret Meade, a small group of dedicated individuals working together can change the world.

Structural systems
Structural engineering is an essential part of designing buildings that lift the spirit (as well as keeping the building aloft). Structure is so fundamental to architecture that without it, designs are mere fantasies on paper. Conceiving structural systems is therefore a basic and critical element of the preliminary architectural design process. Just as with movement systems, structural systems can impart order and help to organize spaces in the building. So, the message is that structural components such as columns—their locations, bay size, and so on—must be delineated on those early conceptual sketches. Cross-sections, revealing depth of spanning members (beams, girders), are influenced by column locations. Drawing the structural elements facilitates lining up the load-bearing elements from one floor to the next, which is an efficient way to handle gravity loads.

To put the structural system in perspective, according to structural engineer Herman Spiegel,[33] "If the structural engineering accounts for 20 to 30 percent of a building, it will have profound influences on the design, the aesthetics, the manipulation of all the resources to make the most beautiful project." The good news is that, structurally, just about anything is possible. The bad news is that the more structural gymnastics are required, the greater likelihood that schemes will be prohibitively expensive. For example, the addition or strategic placement of a column to obviate the need for a huge cantilever could save thousands of dollars in construction costs and engineering fees. But, pushing the design envelope and the engineering consultant to innovate in support of the architectural intention is usually in the best interests of the project. It behoves the architect to balance available resources with any proposed structural ideas. Pioneering structural engineers include Robert Maillart, Pier Luigi Nervi, and Félix Candela. Other distinguished engineers include Peter Rice, Santiago Calatrava, William LeMessurier, and Fazlur Kahn.

"There is nothing more discouraging to an engineer than to work with an architect who either has adopted a very conservative structural approach requiring the engineer to do nothing more than size the beams and columns, or has no idea how to make the structural system work and hopes that the engineer will magically solve the problem," says Vienna, Virginia structural engineer Denis J. McMullan, PE.[34] He suggests that the architect and engineer conduct mini-workshops early in the design process to avoid the traps just noted. The mini-workshops or brainstorming sessions—whatever they may be—should occur face-to-face and include all the building systems consultants for a rich and stimulating dialogue to ensure the systems' compatibility and synergy.

Another factor in conceiving the structural system is its contribution to the environmental sensitivity of the project. For example, masonry-bearing walls can provide a significant thermal mass for passive heating and cooling. At the other end of the spectrum, light-weight wood framing is sensitive to temperature changes and has an application for hot, humid climates.

Structure may be expressed or concealed depending on the architectural intent, i.e., physically integrated—or not—with other systems. For example, a roof supported by a symmetrical array of columns can be independent of the cladding on an asymmetrical pavilion beneath it. The Heidi Weber House in Zürich illustrates this point. It is a museum dedicated to the work of Le Corbusier and consists of a pavilion that sits beneath a structurally independent prefabricated steel roof.

Mete Turan, Ph.D.,[35] professor at Roger Williams University, submits that structural design is composed of form-making and computation. He says: "One is intuitive, subjective, and synthetic; the other is rational, objective, and analytical." The best structural engineering is a union of, or dialogue between, the two. Turan concludes: "Generation of structural form begins with knowledge of the basic structural systems and their components, materials and their inherent properties, and the forces to which a structure must respond."

Mechanical systems
Environmental controls, including HVAC, should be thought of as integral to the early stages of design. Buildings consume a huge percentage of energy resources. One explanation for this may lie in the failure to focus on integration of environmental systems with design concepts at the very beginning of the design process.

Figure 3.37
Bell Canada Enterprises Place, Gallery & Heritage Square in Toronto designed by Santiago Calatrava with Skidmore, Owings & Merrill. The six-storey gallery connects two towers with a white painted steel and glass passageway. The exposed modern tree-like form has associations with the Gothic tradition, and is a stunning structural exhibition.

Carl Bovill[36] highlights a key point in examining systems at the earliest stages of a project: "For the creative manipulation of the HVAC implications in architectural design the architect needs to consider the relationship between spatial organization, structural requirements, and the HVAC needs in an overall way. In order for this to happen at the highest levels of design intent, detail must be suppressed and strategic concept emphasized." Here's an outrageous proposal that exemplifies this way of thinking: Use supporting structure for plumbing; steel tube pipe columns would perform double duty as plumbing lines. This may sound incongruous, but represents the kind of early investigation of technological concepts that develops understanding of building systems and creative problem-solving.

A hybrid, three-tier approach to the design of HVAC and lighting systems is advocated by Norbert Lechner,[37] author of *Heating, Cooling, Lighting: Sustainable Design Methods for Architects*. This approach, encapsulated as follows, is especially salient for the schematic design phase.

Tier 1, basic building design. Issues such as orientation, degree of compactness of the form, size and location of fenestration, shading systems, envelope construction, materials, colors, and so on are addressed to minimize the need for heating, cooling, and lighting. These are all factors in sizing and selecting mechanical systems, and, handled sensitively, can reduce equipment sizes.

Tier 2, passive systems. Natural energy sources are used for passive heating, passive cooling, and daylighting. Passive heating strategies use south-facing windows and clerestories along with thermal mass to collect and store excess solar heat collected during the winter day for nighttime use. Passive cooling strategies include the use of wind for comfort ventilation or convective cooling, the use of water for evaporative cooling, and the use of radiators for nighttime radiant cooling. Daylighting strategies bring good-quality daylight into the building to make it possible to turn off the electric lights during most of the daytime hours.

Tier 3, mechanical equipment. Buildings fully utilizing the strategies of Tiers 1 and 2 will in most cases still require some mechanical equipment, but the size, cost, and energy demands of this equipment will then be comparatively small. The art and science of coordinating the building envelope design with HVAC requirements such that these systems work together to amplify efficiency is the essence of well-conceived mechanical system design. Noteworthy is a similar approach to the marriage of fenestration, glazing, and interior electric lighting.

Lechner suggests that the following—related to mechanical equipment—should be considered in schematic design because of their spatial and aesthetic implications:

- sizing and locating mechanical equipment rooms;
- exposing or hiding the ductwork;
- establishing floor-to-floor heights and clearances with the structure for the ductwork;
- locating intake and exhaust louvers on exterior walls;
- locating the condenser unit (cooling tower) on the roof or on grade next to the building;
- deciding whether to use solar collector panels, photovoltaics, windpower, and so on.

Lighting

There is no end to the possibilities of light—for it is the source of magic in architecture. I believe that light is the ultimate determinant of design. I am convinced that how we see things as a consequence of light is fundamental to the formation of human perception and imagination.

Arthur Erickson[38]

In the quote above, Erickson captures some of the more intangible and even biological correlates of lighting. Lighting is truly a multidimensional field that legitimately contains as much metaphysics as it does physics.

William Lam was one of the pioneers in the relatively new specialty of architectural lighting. His classic books, *Perception and Lighting as Formgivers for Architecture* (McGraw-Hill, 1977) and *Sunlighting as Formgiver for Architecture* (Van Nostrand Reinhold, 1986), emphasize the importance of lighting in the design process, elaborate theoretical concepts, and illustrate practical design methods and their application to projects.

Lam[39] has discussed what he finds most frustrating about the way in which projects are developed in terms of lighting. He speaks of a natural but dangerous sort of nearsightedness from which many practitioners seem to suffer: "Designers often start by focusing only upon some parts of the design challenge." The problem, Lam believes, is compounded by the order in which lighting is considered. He observes that there is the tendency to design the structure in relation to the plan, then the mechanical systems, *and then* lighting—in that sequence. The systems become add-ons rather than part of an initial concept. Lam urges that architects try to conceive of all the issues from the first efforts to develop a design solution. Imagination then is not limited and the process becomes an integrative one rather than one of erosion.

Lam has talked persuasively about lighting in relation to the design process. He characterizes the potential impact of good lighting: "to facilitate orientation, to provide focus, sparkle, even essential character of a space, and to satisfy fundamental biological needs for view and for sun as well as for the activity needs." Keeping all this in mind, Lam implores that we "ask the right questions about the spaces to be designed—just what are the qualities you want?" Lam mandates that we think about lighting early and start with diagramming early:

Diagrammatic sections especially can be readily used to explore design concepts and develop designs in advance of model building. Sketch lines of illumination and probable reflection and glare. It's amazing how well the diagrams can help catalog real conditions and in turn lead one to good concepts for lighting, which can then be tested in a model.

In learning about lighting design, Lam advises designers to know why things are perceived the way they are:

If you know what a good environment is, you can design one. Think concept first, hardware last. Think about what wants to be lit, why, and how it should appear. Think and diagram in three dimensions. Diagram light in relation to architectural features, artwork, furnishings, and the projected activities in the space, and then where the light may come from. The reflected ceiling plan comes last.

Sculpting interior space—creating planes, for example, for bouncing light and pockets to conceal light sources or washing surfaces with light—are strategies to reduce glare and create a soft, diffuse, ambient light for general illumination. When supplemented with a suitable amount of direct light for specific tasks (and a bit of sparkle), a synergistic fit with function and architectural features begins to take shape. Surface color is an important consideration; promoting reflections or reducing glare are all part of the design picture (see Figure 2.27).

Howard Brandston,[40] an acclaimed lighting designer, discusses good lighting design in his book *Learning to See: A Matter of Light*. He says that a good lighting design is realized if:

- All spaces (e.g., entry, transition, linger, work, and exit) are properly composed in a clear hierarchy of importance and purpose.
- The lighting provides spatial clarity.
- The lighting mood is consistent with the function and design of each space.
- It promotes productivity.
- It is within the user's budget.
- It has fully utilized the potential of daylight when available.
- It is readily maintainable.
- It is energy-effective.
- All state-of-the-art alternatives have been considered.

So what else should architects be aware of as they consider the preliminary design of lighting systems? Charles Linn, FAIA,[41] responded: "The ways in which the lighting will affect the mood and feel of interior spaces is something that architects must learn to be aware of as they design, just as they become aware of building materials, texture, color, and other design elements." Linn specifies how to do just that:

> Make a point to look at lighting. Go into stores, churches, office buildings, museums, or out on the street and observe the lighting. Look at what fixtures are like and what they do. What color is the light? What are the shadow patterns like? Does the light make harsh shadows, or is it diffuse? What is the light source? What is the color rendering of the light? Does it make the skin look rosy or pale or green?

Answering these questions will help you to really see the light and its design.

Acoustics

The acoustical environment represents a design opportunity that should be consciously exploited as an integral part of the design process. Typically, when the acoustical qualities of a room are satisfactory for its programmed function, the design strategies will be undetected. If ignored in design, acoustics may not be well suited to the functions in a given space and significantly detract from the architecture.

To take full advantage this design opportunity, architects must learn about applying some essential principles of the physics of sound and the physiology of hearing. Moreover, Gary Siebein,[42] an acoustical consultant and professor at the University of Florida, talks about designing rooms to make sounds poetic. He says: "A room can enhance sounds within it the same way that the wooden body of an acoustic guitar or violin enhances the vibrations of the strings." So reverberation is a key acoustical quality; it is the persistence of a sound in a room after the source has stopped due to repeated reflections from room surfaces. Excessive reverberation in a lecture room makes it difficult to understand the speaker. Short reverberation time, on the other hand, facilitates hearing the articulated, clear sounds of speech. Some reverberation, however, may "enhance" a lecturer's performance. In contrast to speech, symphony performances benefit from longer reverberation times for an artful mixing of sounds of the various instruments.

Reverberation time is not the primary issue, however, in conference rooms, corporate board rooms, and classrooms, according to Mark Holden[43] of JaffeHolden. The way in which sound reflects from the room's surfaces is more important. He says: "Achieving the correct reflection patterns for sound in a small space is the key to proper room acoustics. The designer has many tools that can be used to control, angle, direct, absorb, reflect, or diffuse sound within a room." Tools include materials selections such as acoustical tile and carpet and room size and proportions. The reflective properties of a room can be used to amplify sound so that it is heard from those reflections as well as directly from the source. Edward Allen[44] describes a situation in which "the ceilings of meeting rooms, classrooms, and auditoriums sometimes are completely covered with sound-absorbing materials by well-intentioned but ill-informed people. This nullifies the potential for sound reinforcement offered by reflections off the ceiling, resulting in inadequate sound l evels toward the rear of the room."

Shape, volume, and materials all contribute to the acoustical character of a space. For example, concave surfaces such as domes focus sound reflections resulting in both loud and quiet areas. Convex surfaces as well as rooms with irregular geometry, on the other hand, diffuse sounds everywhere in the space. Long, narrow spaces with parallel surfaces that reflect sound can create unpleasant persistence of sounds. Gary Siebein explains that sounds persist longer in rooms that have larger volumes, and that excessive reverberation can typically occur in office building atria, church halls, restaurants, and even great rooms in residences.

The type of acoustical environment required for each activity in the building will help to inform design thinking. For example, a library reading room should be a quiet space for concentration. Siebein[45] comments:

> one way to achieve this quality is to design a room with a low ceiling and to line the room with absorbent materials. Another way to achieve the same result would be to design a high ceiling and line the room with hard materials. Any sounds made in this room would be heard loudly throughout the room. This would make people more conscious of the noise they make and would also result in a quiet room.

Another example is how loud noise in a restaurant can be considered a positive quality because it allows for private conversations or babies crying without disturbing patrons.

There are some fairly straightforward planning and organizational strategies that can have a big influence on acoustics. In terms of the site, as part of a rigorous site analysis, log time during the course of a day (and try to extrapolate for variations during the year) to ascertain noisy and quiet areas, including positive attributes such as waves crashing on a shore, birds chirping, leaves rustling in the wind, etc., and negatives such as traffic noise, music blaring from a neighbor, an air-handling unit on an adjacent property, etc. Zone quiet activities in

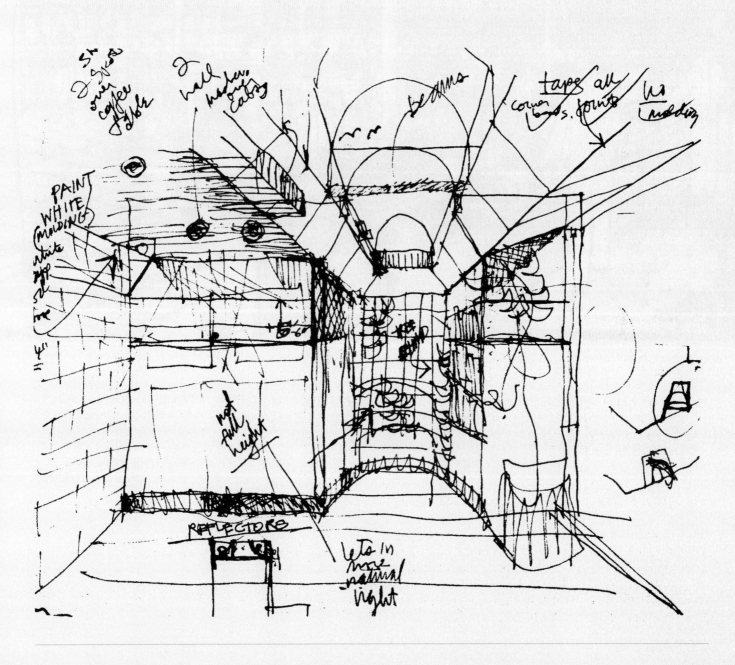

Figure 3.38
A doodle of a new family room,
presented to the client, conveys
the basic elements of the design—
skylight, splayed ceiling forms,
rounded glass block terminus.

Figure 3.39
Samsung Senior Intelligent
Town project. The loose sketch
beautifully communicates the
feeling of the public gathering
space (project by David W.
Vaughan with Nikken Sekkei
Architects, © David W. Vaughan).

the building away from noisy areas on the site. Isolate spaces in the building that support noisy or quiet activities. Employ buffer spaces such as closets and corridors to contribute to the separation of noisy from quiet zones.

There are construction details to limit airborne or structure-borne noise transmission such as airtight sealing of all openings in partitions, using resilient metal clips instead of screws to attach gypsum board to framing, double stud walls, and so on. Massive, impervious materials or assemblies such as walls made of brick or multiple layers of gypsum board help to acoustically separate spaces by controlling sound transmission. In contrast, lightweight, porous materials help to control reverberation.

Masking sounds is another strategy to obviate noise problems. Masking sources can be fabricated electronically (i.e., in an open office context) or have a more natural feeling (i.e., a fountain in an atrium or urban context).

Equipment in mechanical rooms can be a source of noise and vibration that needs to be controlled. Vibration isolators on the equipment, duct silencers, flexible connections to reduce vibration transmission, sound-absorbing duct lining, appropriately sized ducts (smaller ducts mean increased air velocity, which is noisy), wide-radius elbows and transitions to facilitate smooth airflow, and so on are examples of noise-reduction strategies. These strategies may have an impact on sizing the mechanical room, which has implications for schematic design.

Preliminary design presentations

Effectively presenting design schemes to a client is a key step in the design process. Great work ends up on the cutting-room floor if a client does not perceive that it is great. Charles Gwathmey[46] eloquently makes the point: "If you include the client in an understanding of the problem and how you are responding to it, it makes the solution understandable instead of a mysterious aesthetic proposition. Issues of taste go away."

One way to operationalize Gwathmey's suggestion is to share the design process with the client. That is, present and discuss initial sketches, images, and study models that were used to test ideas and make design decisions. There is a personal and alluring quality to those original process materials that can be quite persuasive (see Figures 3.38 and 3.39). Moreover, realistic three-dimensional representations of the work greatly facilitate a client's understanding of the project. Plans and sections are not always easy for the non-architect to read—it takes considerable effort and time to coordinate and assimilate the different pieces of information contained therein. Marc Hinshaw[47] perceptively observed, "The model is there to comfort the client so that the drawings can reach for a higher level of understanding about a project. It is like a one-two punch."

If you know what you're talking about, and can say it directly to your audience (i.e., with as much eye contact as possible), you will radiate confidence. Try not to patronize people by an exaggerated or simplified lecture; encourage questions and respond with a level of detail consistent with the inquiry, but without jargon. John Lyons, Ph.D.,[48] states:

> The key to a presentation, whether it's before a small-town client or the
> Congress of the United States, is to define what you want to say. One or two
> points should be identified, and those are the ones you amplify. More than

Sidebar 3.4: Tips for presentations

Include context and entourage (i.e., people, trees, cars, and so on) within which the building sits to make it come to life, impart a sense of scale, and tie it to the surroundings. Set the building in a place, whether adjacent to other buildings or landscape, and include foreground and background. Losing touch with reality by employing a stylized or caricatured approach to entourage risks misrepresenting design ideas.

Communication is almost always enhanced when ideas are graphically expressed for the non-architect (i.e., realistically, three-dimensionally). Better design more than likely follows from improved dialogue between architect and client.

Share process drawings with the client. They show how the project evolved, how some key decisions were made, and perhaps how the client's input was incorporated into the project.

Keep an eye on size and scale when drawing by hand. Working smaller can save a lot of time. The drama of large scale can then be achieved by digital means (see Figure 3.40).

Drawings are read and appreciated far more easily when there is a standard orientation. This tip is almost too obvious: Neighborhood, site, and floor plans should all have the same orientation, and include a north arrow.

Align floor plans as they would appear in reality (i.e., a stair tower should appear in the same relative location on all plans, even if the shapes of the plans are different).

Provide a sense of scale in the drawings with a suggested furnishings layout in both plan and section (in addition to including a graphic scale). This shows that the specific functioning of the space has been thoughtfully considered.

In general, attempt to present plans, elevations, and sections at the same scale. It makes it easier to compare drawings.

Key all cross-sections, elevations, and perspectives to the presentation plans for easy reference by clients.

Elevation labels usually refer to the cardinal directions of the compass (i.e., the east elevation faces east). Some clients occasionally incorrectly perceive the elevation as the direction in which they are viewing it.

Keep sheet format simple. Avoid overly stylized graphic or other idiosyncratic elements; they draw attention away from the architectural project. You don't want a selection committee discussing some obscure element at the expense of your design.

Employ a hierarchy of line weights to highlight (by contrast) more important elements. They can also help to give a sense of depth. If everything is equally weighted and there is no hierarchy, nothing reads prominently.

Use shade and shadow liberally. These qualities add depth, texture, and contrast to emphasize and animate forms, imbue two-dimensional drawings with a sense of reality, and help them to read better at a distance. On occasion, grant yourself artistic license in developing shade and shadows to improve clarity, but be consistent within a set of drawings.

In floor plans, use the convention of dotted lines to indicate space above (i.e., overhangs, balconies, floors, etc.). This helps in comparing and reading plans and sections.

Suggest materials. Partially render rather than draw every brick, for example. Concentrate the texture or value at the edges, and gradually diminish the density so it doesn't dominate the drawing.

Generally, provide more detail in the foreground, less in the background. Overlapping objects or cutting elements (i.e., only the upper half of a person is visible behind a counter) enhance the illusion of depth.

Figure 3.40
These preliminary design sketches of a gymnasium were drawn quickly at 8" x 10" and enlarged to a dramatic 30" x 40". The ink drawings were especially amenable to zooming in.

this and most people tend to become ineffective and lose their audience. Present with confidence. Self-confidence is a most important metric of the effective presentation. The worst thing presenters do is to become their own audience, to get idiosyncratic. Stay basic, stay confident, and keep it brief. There will always be time to elaborate if that is called for.

The overarching message is to project confidence if not charisma, express enthusiasm and excitement, "grab" the audience, and enjoy the experience.

Another useful perspective is to view the application of negotiating skills as a tool for discussions about design. Negotiating skills are essential for conducting business, but can also be used as an integral part of the arsenal of presentation tools. Harvard Professor of Management Practice, Michael Wheeler,[49] states: "People can feel possessive about an idea—or bargaining position. Good negotiators recognize this and find ways to let people save face so that they don't feel they've been stripped of their possessions, including their self-respect." Excellent negotiating skills can be relevant to educating and selling a client on design possibilities. Of particular note for designers is the idea of "principled negotiation," proposed by Roger Fisher and William Ury[50] in their classic book on negotiation *Getting to Yes*, in which they recommend that issues be decided on their merits. An important caveat is to recognize that everyone is (theoretically) on the same team, sharing the same goals. The "negotiation" should then be viewed as a mechanism for mutual understanding and enlightenment toward creating a better project, not as something to win.

Notes on graphics
Preparation for presenting schematic designs to stakeholders should be coincident with the creation of initial design ideas. Always think about how the design proposal will be framed—both graphically and verbally—in terms that will be understandable and exciting to the client. But don't let the notion of effective communication inhibit experimentation in developing the work.

A great presentation of a great design can capture its essence and distinguish you from everyone else who has talent and enthusiasm. The graphics package can count for a lot—at least initially. That is not to say that slickness and sheen are sufficient. It is possible to make a bad design look good with a superior presentation, but what's the point? No one will be fooled in the long run. A good design can look bad by not paying enough attention to professional quality in the presentation. However, be wary of media that turn out to be more of a gimmick, where attention is drawn to the medium and not the design.

Create a focus along with a gradation of values on each presentation drawing or slide. Even a floor plan can have a focus by highlighting a certain element within the plan, for example, the circulation path: A gray tone, or perhaps some color to show the underlying organization. The drawing becomes graphically interesting and easier to read because the viewer's interest is not diffused. Alternatively, emphasize graphically whatever is particularly noteworthy by more detailed rendering so that it becomes the focus.

Using color in presentations is terrific, but only if it enhances the message. Its use shouldn't be arbitrary. If color is an integral part of the project, the presentation demands it. If, however, you're showing something subtle, like a certain species of wood or type of stone, the beauty of it might be in its muted tones—bold color would be inappropriate.

Take direction from the specifics of the design. You don't necessarily need to use a rainbow of colors—one or two might be most effective for any given presentation. A *little bit* of color can have a big impact.

Charrettes and competitions

No discussion about doing design would be complete without describing the great potentials of two tried-and-true mechanisms for promoting and advancing the work. I am a big proponent of using the *charrette*-mode of design to kick off a project. Even though the outcome of a charrette may not resemble the final design, a charrette is an exciting way to dive into the work. It launches the preliminary design phase by actually doing preliminary design as a means to fully grasp all the programmatic, site, budget, and other salient factors; to develop more detailed, relevant questions; and to test preliminary ideas and an overarching vision for the project.

Architectural design competitions involve a similar type of focused immersion as charrettes, but with a typical expectation of producing something fairly well resolved that is unique, innovative, artful, and perhaps culturally significant, at least as a first step in realizing a built outcome. The emphasis on design thinking and fresh ideas is paramount (and, hopefully, rewarded); a luxury that is not always possible on conventional projects.

Both charrettes and competitions require interpretation of a relatively moderate amount of data because of the early stage of the project in the case of a charrette, or due to the fixed initial program and site information for all entrants in the case of a competition. Therefore the designer(s) must make intelligent assumptions about missing information, then translate it to a physical design in order to advance the work.

Charrettes
An excellent process technique to jump-start creative design thinking at the beginning of projects is termed "charrette." Generally, this suggests a total immersion in design investigations in a very compressed, uninterrupted time frame, either independently or in a team context. There are a number of meanings ascribed to the French word, *charrette*. One definition, used at the École des Beaux Arts in Paris during the nineteenth century, describes students' intense efforts to complete projects. *Squatters*, coined by Caudill Rowlett Scott,[51] is synonymous with charrette, and is similarly used to describe a highly focused several-day on-site collaborative work session to develop preliminary design ideas and schemes. Another definition offered by the National Charrette Institute,[52] which is particularly well suited to community planning, describes the charrette as "a collaborative design and planning workshop that … involves all affected stakeholders in a series of feedback loops, resulting in a feasible plan." Whatever it is called, this strategy can be extremely effective, even inspiring, in identifying key issues and in starting design work on a project.

For the purposes of this chapter—to identify ways to facilitate architectural design—a charrette is a dedicated block of time used to brainstorm and design the building schematically *yet completely* (including all systems and materials selections) given the rough framework of the problem. However, there is much flexibility in how and when a charrette can be planned. A charrette should ideally occur at the start of preliminary design but can be deployed at any phase with any special focus. For example, perhaps there is a need to develop construction details midway through the project. A charrette could be designed to focus exclusively on connections, materials, components, and assemblies. The designer who is an expert on the building type could be paired with a very experienced construction detailer in addition to a knowledgeable representative from the contractor and/or the consulting structural engineer.

The charrette can be an individual undertaking; part of an internal (firm or studio) process alone or together with consulting engineers; results may or may not be shared with the client; or the client and other stakeholders may be invited to participate as collaborators. Jordan Goldstein,[53] Managing Director of Gensler's Washington, D.C. office, comments that a charrette, involving a combination of junior and senior people from multiple disciplines, amounts to a bit of "design combustion that focuses the team around a shared vision for success and innovation."

It seems counterintuitive that design work should begin before all of the project information, analyses, and so on are in place. There is great benefit, however, to launching a project in this fashion. Design via charrette is a means to fast-tracking understanding and analyzing the major issues of the project, and to eliciting high-quality and immediate feedback on which to base further design investigations. A charrette allows quick discovery and testing of preliminary concepts and organizational ideas. The results of a charrette provide a starting point for meaningful in-depth discussions with other members of the design team (and possibly the client). It will be very clear what additional information is needed; questions will be reframed, and new ones will be posed to move forward with design schemes.

An example of a building design charrette was the design section of the old National Council of Architectural Registration Boards qualifying exam required for licensure of architects. (This was before there was a computerized exam; candidates brought their own T-squares, triangles, and drawing boards!) There was a continuous 11-hour marathon session during which candidates were given a program and site for a roughly 25,000 square-foot pubic building and were required to design it in a fairly comprehensive way (including program and site analyses, the building design itself including systems development and materials selections, and a graphic presentation with narrative stating the concepts of the solution). The "deliverables" included site plan, floor plans, cross-sections, elevations, and diagrams illustrating environmentally sensitive design strategies, circulation patterns (pedestrian, vehicular, and service), structural, mechanical, and lighting systems.

This was a test of endurance as much as a test of application of design principles ensuring the health, safety, and welfare of the building inhabitants. The example is noteworthy, however, because it demonstrates that, in a very short period of time, it is indeed possible to create a design in holistic fashion with building systems integrated. Two related additional points: (1) (re)design is not that time-intensive at an early stage. Projects can benefit from redesign at this point in the process, and (2) a charrette can be an excellent strategy to generate ideas if one is stuck.

Competitions
Competitions provide opportunities to advance a particular design thesis, experiment with design thinking, enlighten the public, or expand expertise into an unfamiliar building-type. They offer a means to pursue personal design agendas, new technologies, and theoretical concerns that may be inappropriate for typical projects in the office. Indeed, architects can push the design envelope in competitions because competitions encourage an open and

inventive approach to projects.

So, how do architectural design competitions "facilitate" design? Ideas from a competition submission can frequently be used to inform and invigorate work on a conventional project. Therefore, time spent on competitions is a worthwhile investment; even losing schemes can enhance a firm's marketing portfolio, particularly in difficult economic cycles. Moreover, competitions provide a chance for small, evolving firms to engage large-scale projects because in theory, competitions provide the possibility to secure commissions on pure merit.

Competitions are criticized, on one hand, because the process is inherently flawed: There is no dialogue between client and architect. On the other hand, the deliverables for the competition help distill the issues and set the stage for a fresh dialogue with all stakeholders after the architect is subsequently selected.

It is important to understand the competition's rules regarding intellectual property. Typically, the architect owns the "Instruments of Service" and grants the sponsor a nonexclusive license to publish and display submission drawings and models. If this is not the case, then move on. We shouldn't give away our most valuable assets: Creative ideas.

Collaboration with colleagues might be a good tactic to optimize benefits and minimize liabilities on a submission entry to a competition. Experience working in a team context is quite valuable and perhaps can be leveraged for qualification on another project. Exposure to critical dialogue as a consequence of working with colleagues can be energizing, and can result in a more thoughtful design process. Collaboration can also reduce individual time and expense commitments required to complete a submission.

Notes

1. Christopher Mead, quoted by the author in "It's not Personal, it's Business: Peer Review and Self-criticism are Crucial Tools that Elevate the Quality of Preliminary Designs," *Architectural Record* vol. 187 no. 9, September 1999, 28.
2. Christopher Mead, "Critical Thinking in Architectural Design," *Architectural Design Portable Handbook*, New York: McGraw-Hill, 2001, pp. 42–44.
3. Geoffrey Adams quoted by the author in "Integrated Practice in Perspective: A New Model for the Architectural Profession," *Architectural Record* vol. 195 no. 5, May 2007, p. 118.
4. William Kirby Lockard, *Drawing as a Means to Architecture*, New York: Van Nostrand Reinhold, 1968, p. 9.
5. Donald A. Schön, *The Reflective Practitioner: How Professionals Think in Action*, New York: Basic Books, 1983, p. 103.
6. Jean Pike, personal communication with the author, March 2000.
7. Robert Hull quoted in "Drawing the Line," by Cheryl Weber, *Residential Architect* vol. 12 no. 7, August 2008, p. 30.
8. Patrycja Doniewski quoted in "Drawing the Line," by Cheryl Weber, *Residential Architect* vol. 12 no. 7, August 2008, p. 34.
9. Geoffrey Adams quoted by the author in "Integrated Practice in Perspective: A New Model for the Architectural Profession," *Architectural Record* vol.195 no. 5, May 2007, p. 120.

10. T.J. Meehan, personal communication with the author, June 28, 2010.

11. Mark C. Childs, personal communication with the author, January 23, 2009.

12. Jim Leggitt, personal communication with the author, April 16, 2009.

13. Gordon Cullen, *The Concise Townscape*, New York: Van Nostrand Reinhold, 1961, pp. 7–8.

14. Lawrence Halprin, personal communication with the author, April 21, 1992.

15. Paul Goldberger, "Pushing Classicism to Extremes," *New York Times*, May 17, 1992, p. 33.

16. Don Hanlon, personal communication with the author, January 7, 2011.

17. Kevin Lynch and Gary Hack, *Site Planning*, Third Edition, Cambridge, MA: The MIT Press, 1984, p. 158.

18. Luis Barragán quoted in *The Architecture of Luis Barragán*, by Emilio Ambasz, New York: The Museum of Modern Art, 1976, p. 8.

19. James Stewart Polshek quoted in "Architectural Ethics," by Suzanne Stephens, *Architecture* vol. 81 no. 3, March 1992, p. 76.

20. William Strunk, Jr. and E.B. White, *The Elements of Style*, Second Edition, New York: The Macmillan Company, 1972, p. 59.

21. John Morris Dixon, "Twentieth-Anniversary Scrapbook: The Editor's Observations on Two Decades at P/A," *Progressive Architecture* vol. LXXII no. 13, December 1991, p. 81.

22. Ricardo Legorreta quoted in "Legorreta: The Color of Gold," by Clifford A. Pearson and David Dillon, *Architectural Record* vol. 188 no. 5, May 2000, p. 158.

23. David Childs quoted from a panel discussion, "The Nature of Place," Charlie Rose Show no. 1766, air date November 8, 1996.

24. Ricardo Legorreta quoted in "Legorreta: The Color of Gold," by Clifford A. Pearson and David Dillon, *Architectural Record* vol. 188 no. 5 May 2000, p. 158.

25. Deborah Sussman quoted in "Working with Color Consultants," by Nancy B. Solomon, *Architecture* vol. 81 no. 1 January 1992, p. 82.

26. Deborah Sussman, personal communication with the author, June 26, 1992.

27. Edward Allen and Joseph Iano, *The Architect's Studio Companion: Rules of Thumb for Preliminary Design*, Fourth Edition, Hoboken, NJ: John Wiley & Sons, 2007.

28. Leonard R. Bachman, *Integrated Buildings: The Systems Basis of Architecture*, Hoboken, NJ: John Wiley & Sons, 2003, pp. 4–16.

29. Yann Weymouth quoted in "Round Table: The Engineering Education of the Architect," by Walter F. Wagner, *Architectural Record* vol. 169 no. 11, mid-August 1981, p. 89.

30. Carl Bovill, *Architectural Design: Integration of Structural and Environmental Systems*, New York: Van Nostrand Reinhold, 1991, pp. 176–77.

31. John C. Maxwell, *The 17 Indisputable Laws of Teamwork*, Nashville, TN: Thomas Nelson, 2001.

32. http://teamstepps.ahrq.gov and www.ahrq.gov/teamsteppstools/instructor/essentials/ (both accessed on May 18, 2011).

33. Herman Spiegel, quoted in "Round Table: The Engineering Education of the Architect," by Walter F. Wagner, *Architectural Record* vol. 169 no. 11, mid-August 1981, p. 82.

34. Denis J. McMullan, personal communication with the author, March 4, 1992.

35. Mete Turan, "Poetics of Structures: Force Follows Form," *Architectural Design Portable Handbook*, New York: McGraw-Hill, 2001, pp. 343, 360.

36. Carl Bovill, *Architectural Design: Integration of Structural and Environmental Systems*, New York: Van Nostrand Reinhold, 1991, p. 87.

37. Norbert Lechner, *Heating, Cooling, Lighting: Sustainable Design Methods for Architects*, Third Edition, Hoboken, NJ: John Wiley & Sons, 2009.

38. Arthur Erickson, *The Architecture of Arthur Erickson*, Vancouver, British Columbia: Douglas & McIntyre Ltd., 1988, pp. 19–20.

39. William M.C. Lam, interview by the author, Cambridge, MA, November 1994.

40. Howard M. Brandston, *Learning to See: A Matter of Light*, New York: Illuminating Engineering Society of North America, 2008, p. 77.

41. Charles Linn, personal communication with the author, January 23, 1991.

42. Gary W. Siebein, personal communication with the author, July 17, 1992.

43. Mark Holden, "Acoustics for Small Spaces," *Progressive Architecture* vol. LXXII no. 4, April 1991.

44. Edward Allen, *How Buildings Work: The Natural Order of Architecture*, Second Edition, New York: Oxford University Press, 1995, p. 129.

45. Gary W. Siebein, personal communication with the author, July 17, 1992.

46. Charles Gwathmey quoted in "Chapter 3: Schematic Design," by Bradford Perkins, *Emerging Professional's Companion*, Washington, D.C.: AIA and NCARB, 2004, p. 3.

47. Marc Hinshaw quoted in "Presenting Ideas," by Thomas Fisher, *Progressive Architecture* vol. LXX no. 6, June 1989, p. 88.

48. John Lyons quoted in "The Presentation," *Architecture 101: A Guide to the Design Studio*, New York: John Wiley & Sons, 1993, p. 133.

49. Michael Wheeler quoted in "You Play the Mall Developer," *Harvard Magazine*, March–April 2004, http://harvardmagazine.com/2004/03/you-play-the-mall-develo.html (accessed on May 18, 2011).

50. Roger Fisher and William Ury, *Getting to Yes: Negotiating Agreement Without Giving In*, Second Edition, New York: Penguin Books, 1991.

51. William W. Caudill, *Architecture by Team: A New Concept for the Practice of Architecture*, New York: Van Nostrand Reinhold, 1971, pp. 311–18.

52. National Charrette Institute (principal authors: Bill Lennertz and Aarin Lutzenhiser), *The Charrette Handbook: The Essential Guide for Accelerated, Collaborative Community Planning*, Chicago, IL: American Planning Association, 2006, p. 176.

53. Jordan Goldstein quoted by the author in "It's a Very Good Time to Develop your Firm's Collaboration Skills," *Architectural Record* vol. 197 no. 4, p. 48.

Chapter 4
Case studies

Case studies can bring to life the shared experiences of both professionals and their clients. The three case studies presented here serve to organize, analyze, and summarize a huge spectrum of historical information and thematic material arising from representative projects. The style of presentation for each of the cases— a small-scale residential job, a new academic building on a university campus, and a division headquarters in an existing suburban office building—reflects the overall flavor of the respective project. For example, the intensely personal nature of the residential project that focuses on interactions between a small handful of individuals (who are spending their own money) contrasts with the more objective, business like feel of the university project with its multitude of stakeholders. But, the common thread linking the three cases is an analysis of the core components of the design process, and how cognitive process elements, architectural concept, and personal vision all interact to produce excellent (award-winning) architecture.

The case studies reveal how disparate elements, from prosaic to the poetic, are integrated into a rational process to demonstrate a gestalt. The process is clearly different for each case, and is driven by the specifics of the circumstance. The circumstance determines the extent to which the components are prioritized and perhaps expressed in the design.

I hope that the detail presented in the case studies will be sufficient to help readers identify with the architects to the extent that they can imagine assuming the challenge of designing the building themselves—and to stimulate creative and critical thinking. As you consider each design problem, it will be evident that there are many possible solutions—not just those proposed by the architects in the cases. Finally, the case studies are intended to show application of material from all three previous chapters to real-life situations, and to recognize the richness and value of a rational design process.

New England residence

Architect: *Andrew Pressman, FAIA; Raymond Novitske, AIA, Associated Architect.* Structural Engineer: *McMullen & Associates, Inc.* General Contractor: *Jeb's Construction, Mark Remignanti.*

My cell phone did its generic warble and vibrate and I reflexively answered with an effort at professional demeanor. The voice on the other end introduced herself as Alexandra, the wife of an old college buddy. Following a second of frantic memory search, I recalled a tall, capable guy who seemed destined for success on Wall Street. Alexandra continued: "We'd like to hire you to design our vacation home in southern Maine." She proceeded to elaborate, plunging into her agenda. "We'd like something contemporary yet traditional, spacious yet intimate, keeping in mind a fairly tight budget, and most importantly a design that evokes memories of summers in Maine when I was a child. Can you design a special place for us?"

"Sure, no problem," was my automatic response, dripping with confidence that I could reconcile the array of seemingly conflicting and impossible-to-achieve general requirements into a work of architecture—all the while privately going through the early stages of dread and doubts about the decision to become an architect in the first place.

"My husband Preston and I have a couple of rough sketches we'd like to show you (see Figure 4.1). Can you meet us at the Starbucks on Route One? It's just a few miles from the site. We can discuss our other wishes and then walk around the property."

Like a puppy dog trying to please its owner, I put on an enthusiastic show and arranged a date and time for coffee. "Looking forward to launching the project," I said, eager for a contract to jump-start my new practice, but feeling increasingly as though I might be making the proverbial deal with the devil.

Washing down a bite of donut with my Blackeye, I asked Alexandra what specifically triggered her nostalgia about the area that might provide a clue for a design concept. She replied: "I love the New England coast, the rugged shoreline, and the bleached houses battered by years of wind, rain, and snow. And there is nothing comparable to sitting around a great big stone fireplace in mid winter, and having intimate conversations with family and close friends."

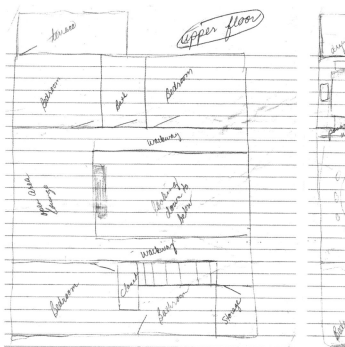
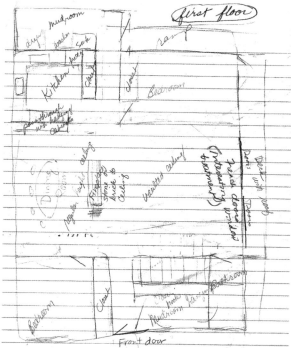

It seemed like this commission was actually going to be worth all the hours of careful cultivation, dialogue, sketching, and model-making: The schematic design was approved by Alexandra and Preston (see Figures 4.3, 4.4, and 4.5). "Okay, Andrew, why don't you go ahead and complete the drawings for construction. We want to use the house this summer. Oh, by the way, Mark, my cousin," Alexandra continued, "will be building the house. He lives about 45 minutes north of our site. And you know that his parents live just down the street from the site—you've met them right? They will be able to keep me posted frequently as building progresses."

About two weeks later, as I had just started the construction documents, Alexandra and Preston suddenly asserted that the entire front (west) elevation, with its shed roof, was "too angular and severe" (see bottom of Figure 4.5). Moreover, they suggested that a gable roof would be preferable to them. They also felt secure in their new feelings since Alexandra's cousin, Mark, who was also going to be the general contractor, was quoted as proclaiming he could build anything without a problem, and implicitly suggested that the addition of his sensibilities—which included design—could only improve upon the final result. The aforementioned parents of Mark compounded the problem by trying to influence the

Figure 4.1 (top)
Initial floor plan sketches provided by the client.
The spatial relationships in the final design very closely approximate those envisioned by the client as depicted in these diagrams.

Figure 4.2 (bottom)
The long, narrow site (looking west) suggested the l inear flow of the house.

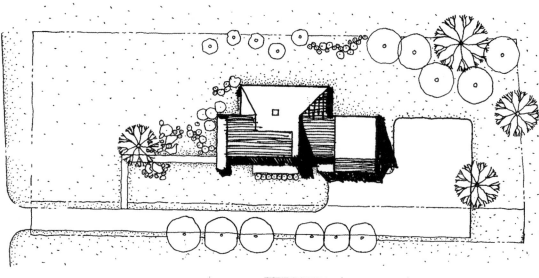

Figure 4.3
Schematic design drawings.
(Top) site plan, (middle) floor
plans, and (bottom) bubble
diagram beginning to translate
client's sketches (from Figure
4.1) to a schematic scheme
(north is up).

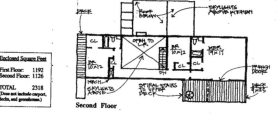

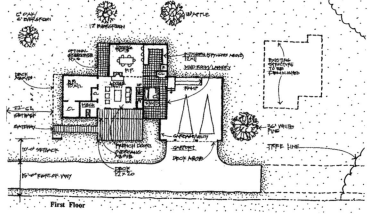

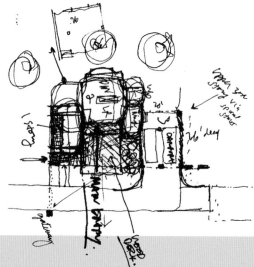

susceptible Alexandra and Preston: "We don't want one of those modern monsters in our backyard. Please ask the architect to tone it down a bit."

I was stunned, no, mortified. I gathered myself, managing to maintain a calm exterior knowing the changes they suddenly desired would destroy the entire design concept of a series of shed roofs pitched in alternate directions toward special views and light (see bottom of Figure 4.6). The magic of the interior spaces and exterior massing would be gone forever. I managed to say that I would give all this careful study and provide my reaction and recommendations in writing.

After a long jog under the hot mid-afternoon sun, I vowed due diligence and reviewed my documentation of the project thus far.

I called Alexandra and cheerily arranged a conference call with her and Preston for the following day, after they'd received the written rationale I'd prepared.

I began the conversation by thanking them for sitting down with me to discuss their prospective changes. My attitude was positive from the start: "You guys are absolutely right—when you look at the elevation as depicted in the drawings, it does appear severe. However, let me point out that elevation drawings are invariably misleading; you know they're really for construction purposes. If you were to perceive, appreciate, and experience all the volumes in reality, you would readily see that the overall composition and massing does in fact create a balanced whole, with the ridge line of the roof as the center of the house, flanked by the dining room/kitchen on one side and the living room and bedrooms on the other. I continued: "So, you see, there is a structural and visual consistency between the exterior configuration and the internal functions with comparable internal volumes. There is also a special focus in this three-dimensional composition: The double-height living room with its roof sloping down to the dining room" (see top of Figure 4.6 and bottom of Figure 4.9).

Figure 4.4
Perspective sketches of the initial scheme that were presented to the client.

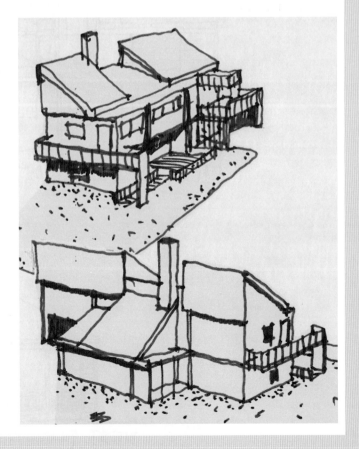

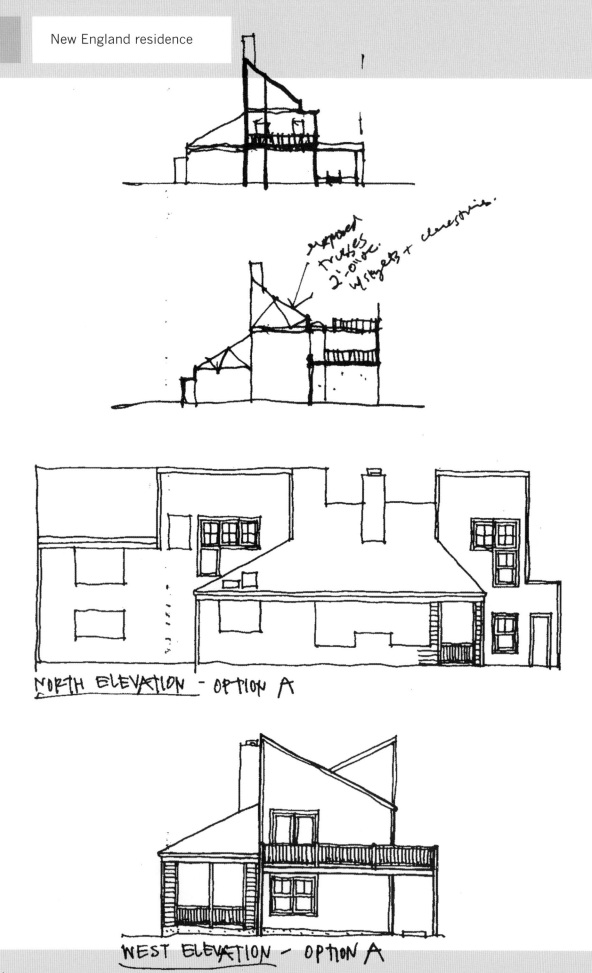

exposed trusses 2'-0" o.c. w/ rafters + clerestories.

NORTH ELEVATION – OPTION A

WEST ELEVATION – OPTION A

Figure 4.5
Schematic design drawings. (Top) cross
sections and (bottom) elevations. The
west elevation, which faces the street, was
the one that was perceived by the clients
to be too "severe."

I allowed a few beats of silence, and looking at their faces it was obvious that Alexandra and Preston weren't there yet. I elaborated: "Let's examine this from another side: If we sliced the top off the existing design and created a gable, the structure immediately becomes more complicated and therefore more expensive to build (not to mention additional fees for the structural engineer and for other design revisions); more support would be required for the new ridge, the ceilings would be lower, and the clerestory windows would be lost, thereby reducing the light and airy feeling of the interior spaces." This time I pushed on without a pause to fully illuminate this perspective: "If the peak in the front bedroom is sliced, then *all* the others must be modified in the same way, otherwise two distinct and opposing aesthetics emerge, which fight with each other. Are you guys understanding my point?"

With somewhat encouraging responsiveness they both chimed in affirmatively. "Give us a day or two to think about this," said Alexandra, ending the meeting.

On the phone the following day, Alexandra and Preston said that while they still felt that the design was too severe and contemporary, they didn't want to pay the additional fees nor delay the schedule. It was a decision based solely on money and time—not design. While an unsatisfactory resolution for me, I was nonetheless confident that they would grow to love the house—particularly when they experienced it in three-dimensional reality.

The construction phase was thankfully rather uneventful. As the building took shape, Alexandra and Preston started smiling and were clearly happy with the built form (see Figure 4.7).

Several months later, I drove to the site to meet a terrific photographer, who agreed to scout the location in preparation for his photo shoot. I brought along several of my own construction progress snapshots I thought would capture the essence of the design. I knew that the best photograph would be an axial photo from the street—the exact same view that was so objectionable to Alexandra and Preston.

I turned into the freshly paved driveway and…gasped with horror. There was a large, newly planted maple tree that blocked the line of sight to the beautiful west elevation (see Figure 4.8). All I could think was: "There goes the magazine cover shot."

Alexandra later explained that, "Without telling us, Mark's parents directed the landscape contractor to plant the biggest tree he could find from a nursery within 50 miles of the site. But it's okay, we actually like it."

At that point I could only shake my head, and keeping a smile on my face, acknowledge that I had satisfied clients and a successful design, and conclude that the position of the tree was not a battle worth fighting. Indeed, any good, robust design ought to be able to endure the insult of a misplaced tree!

Figure 4.6

Cross-sections: (Top) The living room's two-storey ceiling creates drama as it slopes down to the dining room. (Bottom) The shed roof configuration is illustrated, with a similar shed roof pitched in the opposite direction, beyond. Ceilings in the second-floor bedrooms follow the pitch of scissors trusses, allowing enough height for clerestory windows and bunk-beds.

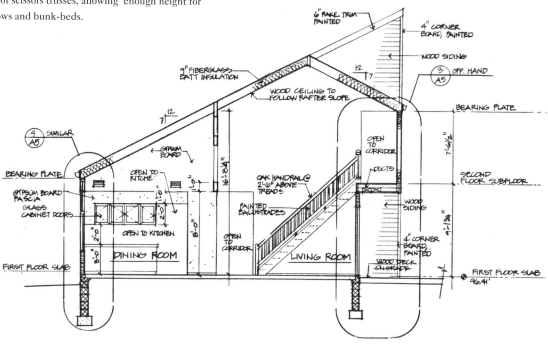

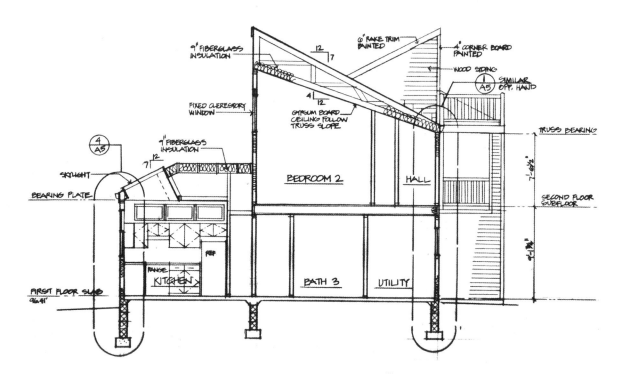

Program summary

A 2,300-square-foot vacation house including four bedrooms, three bathrooms, living room, dining room, kitchen, utility room, numerous outdoor decks, and a two-car garage.

Client preferences

The seemingly contradictory instruction from the client was to "make the design traditional yet contemporary." My interpretation was to fuse the work with the best ideas from traditional New England residential design (i.e., response to climate, use of materials, massing) with a minimal and fundamentally modernist vocabulary. The client also requested that the house convey qualities of light and openness.

Site and context influences

The long, narrow site suggested the linear flow of the house and the elongated rectangle of its plan. There is a 15-foot utility easement running the full length of the site, which doubles as the driveway. The recessed front entry is protected from cold winter winds blowing from the northwest; multiple second-floor decks provide shading from strong afternoon sun in summer. The forms and materials selections were inspired by and built on the local and regional residential design traditions (see bottom image, Figure 4.10). The upper balcony (accessible by spiral stairs from the second floor balcony) abstracts the "widow's walk" often seen in seaboard towns, and provides views to the water.

Architectural concept and organizational ideas

A sequence of shed roofs pitched in alternate directions facilitates the framing of special views, the capture of natural light and breezes, and creates a sculptural massing that is animated but easy to construct. Another idea is to consider the house as a hybrid of a New England farm building and a villa, which acknowledges the surroundings, responds to the client's preferences and program, and generates a distinctive identity.

Designer's agenda

One of the goals—independent of this project's circumstance—was to explore ways to create intriguing yet simple three-dimensional spatial volumes within a coherent overall composition. This had to be accomplished without resorting to complicated or quirky forms.

Figure 4.7 (top)
Construction progress showing framing, sheathing, and some of the fenestration.

Figure 4.8 (bottom)
New maple tree intentionally blocks the line of sight from the street to the west elevation of the new house.

Figure 4.9
(Top) Dining area looking east toward the kitchen, with clerestory windows above wall cabinets in the background. Tops of wall cabinets act as a light shelf, allowing morning light to penetrate deeply into the kitchen. (Bottom) The living room is the heart of the house, with dining and kitchen beyond. The emphasis on soaring volume helps create the feeling of light and openness that the client requested. Note that the pattern of the white beam framing on each side of the fireplace relates to the window pattern in the background (photos © Steve Rosenthal).

Figure 4.10
(Top) The north elevation in late afternoon. Windows that frame special views, fill the interiors with natural light, and capture breezes from multiple directions are below the alternating pitches of the shed roofs. White trim emphasizes the crisp geometry of the three-dimensional forms. (Bottom) Morning view capturing west and south elevations. An influence of the regional context is manifest in massing and clapboard siding, which refer to the coastal vernacular of southern Maine (photos © Steve Rosenthal).

Other critical factors shaping the design

Separate the family's bedrooms on the second floor from the guest bedroom (on the first floor). A missed opportunity involved the design of second-floor bedrooms flanking the upper living room volume. I proposed small interior balconies looking down to the living room below; this would have animated that central space even more, and reinforced it as the heart of the house. Alas, this idea was rejected by the client, who felt that it would compromise privacy.

Cost issues

The mandate from the client for their second home was to "get as much architecture as possible—you know, the hard-to-quantify magical qualities" from a very modest budget. Okay, no problem. The design response was a focus on three-dimensional spatial development rather than specifying expensive materials and finishes.

Materials

Traditional exterior materials such as gray-stained clapboard siding and white trim harmonize with the coastal rural surroundings, and tie the bold forms to the context. Pine plank (ceilings) and granite (fireplace) are available locally.

Building systems

Pre-engineered wood scissors trusses over second-floor bedrooms reinforce the shed roof concept and help to express it on the interior. The ceilings follow the pitch of the bottom chord of the trusses, which provide sufficient volume for clerestory windows and lots of daylight in addition to room for bunk-beds.
This contributes to a feeling of spaciousness, even though the rooms are small (see bottom of Figure 4.6).

Global Heritage Hall

Architect: *Goody Clancy; Roger N. Goldstein, FAIA LEED, Principal*. Structural: *Foley Buhl Roberts & Associates*. Mechanical/Electrical/Plumbing: *Richard D. Kimball Company, Inc.* Landscape: *Carol R. J ohnson Associates, Inc.* Construction Manager: *Shawmut Design and Construction*.

Roger Williams University (RWU) in Bristol, Rhode Island, required over 50,000 gross square feet of new classrooms, faculty offices, and student lounge and interaction spaces. The waterfront site afforded opportunities for dramatic views that were regarded by the client as a clear priority. In fact, capturing and integrating the visually stunning and ever-changing rhythm of the Rhode Island coastal site was intended to serve as the basis of the "campus living room" function. The client recognized that the stimulation from the natural world evokes a range of responses in us from calmness to exhilaration. This was to be their gift to the students. In essence, the architectural challenge was to choreograph light and water within the requirements of the program while respecting the vocabulary of the existing traditional campus.

Program summary
The program comprises approximately 30,000 net square feet (NSF) of space, broken down to approximately 12,700 NSF of classrooms and other instructional spaces; 7,000 NSF of faculty and administrative offices; and 5,000 NSF of interaction and breakout spaces, both enclosed and open, including a major public atrium space. The gross area of the building is approximately 53,000 square feet.

The university wanted this building to not only meet their programmatic needs for classrooms and offices, but to become the "campus living room" where students would gather informally during the course of the day, and where community events would be scheduled, ranging from parties to lectures. The desire for a vibrant, active, high visual impact space within the building was paramount. To the architects, this meant a multi-storey, three-dimensionally exciting space with overlooks from each floor, and views to Mount Hope Bay.

Client preferences
The client clearly wanted the building to fit its context in terms of scale and materials, but they did not dictate a "style" per se. The architects knew from their previous project on campus that the campus standard brick would be expected on this project.

The client articulated a desire for a signature building that would acknowledge and respect the existing campus but signify the university's progress and growth into the new millennium. In addition, there was a request for some expression of the university's commitment to global studies (exemplified in the curriculum by extensive study abroad programs, language programs, and overseas academic affiliations).

Site and context influences

The site's slope toward the bay facilitates the lower level being on grade on one side and the first floor on grade on the opposite side. (See cross-section through atrium, Figure 4.15B.)

The other buildings that frame the quad contiguous to the site are two to three storeys in height, and generally moderate in scale. Most are clad in the campus standard brick or other medium-colored materials. The new building was expected to be a "good neighbor," respecting the scale, materials, and proportions of the architectural precedents on campus.

A campus master plan delineating vehicular and pedestrian circulation was being developed while the building was designed, and the architects supported its intentions in terms of allowing the existing roadway alignment to remain along the west (quad) side of the building, although the hope was that the roadway would eventually be reduced to just a fire lane to make the front of the building more pedestrian-friendly. The main entrance was located off-center relative to the quad in response to the major pathway along the south side of the library. A new plaza, including entrances to the ground floor of the atrium, links to footpaths that run along the waterside of the building between Marine Sciences to the north and the dorms to the south. Finally, service and fire-truck access needed to be from the campus roadway but to be as concealed as possible from view from the quad.

The issue of how best to define the east end of the quad was critically important at the outset of the design process. Should the building close the view or frame it, or some combination thereof?

(A)

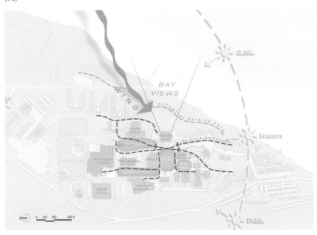

(B)

Figure 4.11

(A) The RWU campus plan. The existing student union, an undistinguished 1960s "block," was demolished for the site of Global Heritage Hall. Most of the construction demolition debris was recycled. The new building sits roughly where the old building was, taking advantage of the excavation zone. (B) Site analysis diagram highlighting view corridor to the bay, solar path, prevailing winds, and pedestrian circulation (courtesy of Goody Clancy).

Architectural concept and organizational ideas

During the initial pre-design phase of the project, the architects worked with a client team that included faculty, administration, facilities staff, and others. Multiple massing and building position options were developed for the client's evaluation. Some options fully closed the quad, revealing water views from the quad on either side of the building. Other options literally framed the view from one or both sides of the view corridor. Ultimately, the preferred option emerged, which then became the basis for the design.

So, the overarching concept was to exploit and dramatize the water view. This is accomplished by: (1) revealing it gradually from the quad with the big curved front facade, then ending with a free-standing column; one's eye is drawn across the building to a framed view. And (2) the building's transparency from west to east as seen through the entry to the atrium gives pedestrians a sense of the view beyond as they approach the building, then, upon entering the building, the water view presents itself to the viewer by way of the atrium volume (see Figure 4.15C).

The programmed spaces are organized in an L-shape surrounding the three-storey glass-walled atrium that focuses on the view. The metal- and glass-clad north wing contains stacked classrooms and the brick-clad curved west wing contains offices. A set of "fin walls" pierces through the building plan expressing a radiating geometry to highlight the bold curve; they are clad with metal panels, both outside and inside. This geometry is overlaid on the L-shape (see plans, Figure 4.14 and elevation, Figure 4.19).

Designer's agenda

The architects wanted to build on their previous experience with the design of classrooms and academic buildings on many other campuses to advance the quality of instructional space, especially for the kinds of simple flat-floor teaching areas called for in this program. Similarly, they wanted to raise the overall quality of design on the RWU campus, applying the same level of creativity demonstrated on their previous building there, the Commons dining facility, but in a different vocabulary.

The architects' agenda included incorporation of sustainable design strategies from the outset, i.e., extensive daylighting, certified wood, operable windows, white roof, efficient light fixtures, and

Figure 4.12

(A) Initial concept sketch developed on the back
of a boarding pass. (B) Concept sketch; note that
structural bay size and columns are evident even at
this very early stage in the design process (courtesy
of Goody Clancy).

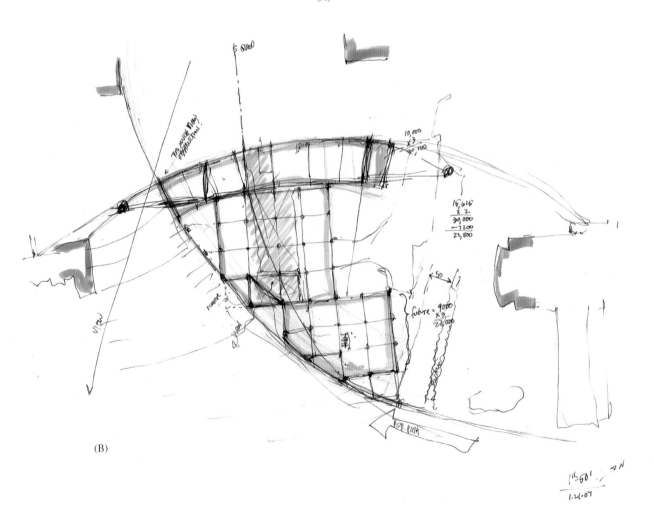

(A)

2. Have a condition, which is not apparent, that would prevent you from performing the duties listed;

3. May suffer bodily harm as a result of performing one or more of the duties listed;

4. Do not wish to perform the exit seat duties in the event of an emergency;

5. Do not speak, read, or understand English.

Emergency Exit Seat Duties

In the event of an emergency in which a crewmember is not available to assist, you may be called upon to perform the following duties:

1. Locate the emergency exit;

2. Recognize the exit opening mechanism;

3. Comprehend the instructions for operating the emergency exit;

4. Assess whether opening the emergency exit will increase the hazards to which passengers may be exposed;

5. Operate the emergency exit;

6. Follow oral directions and hand signals given by a crewmember;

7. Stow or secure the emergency exit door so that it will not hinder use of the exit;

8. Assess conditions of the escape slide, activate the slide and stabilize the slide after deployment to assist others in getting off the slide;

9. Pass quickly through the emergency exit;

10. Assess, select and follow a safe path away from the emergency exit.

Selection Criteria

You may not sit in an exit seat if you are unable to perform the Emergency Exit Seat Duties as described because:

1. You lack sufficient mobility, strength, or dexterity in both arms and hands, and both legs;

(B)

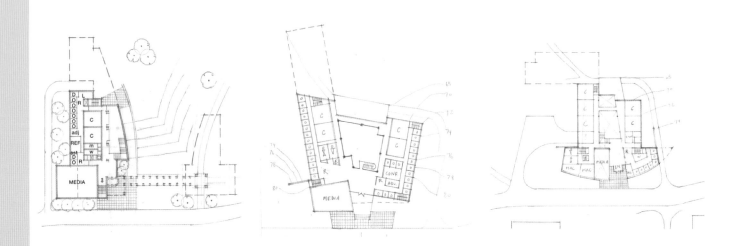

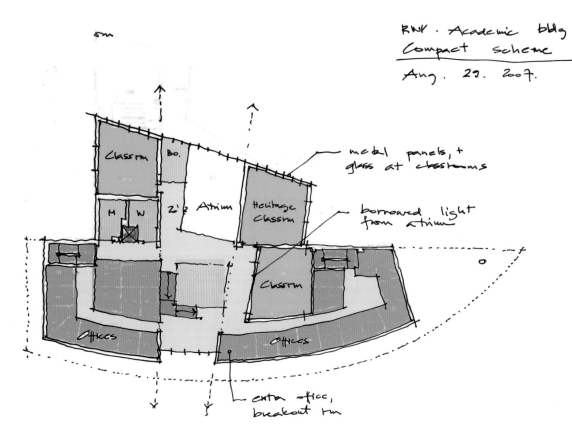

Figure 4.13
Diagrams explore space planning possibilities
(courtesy of Goody Clancy).

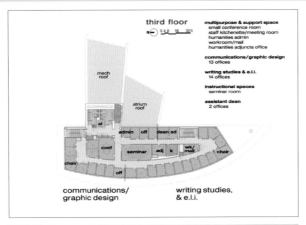

third floor

N ⊙ 0 4 8   16   32ft

multipurpose & support space
small conference room
staff kitchenette/meeting room
humanities admin
workroom/mail
humanities adjuncts office

communications/graphic design
13 offices

writing studies & e.l.i.
14 offices

instructional spaces
seminar room

assistant dean
2 offices

communications/
graphic design

writing studies,
& e.l.i.

second floor

N ⊙ 0 4 8   16   32ft

english & creative writing
10 offices

languages & classics/philosophy
12 offices

multipurpose & support space
workroom
humanities admin

instructional spaces
2 classrooms
1 heritage classroom
1 breakout room
1 breakout area
1 seminar room
1 publications room

english &
creative writing

languages & classics/
philosophy

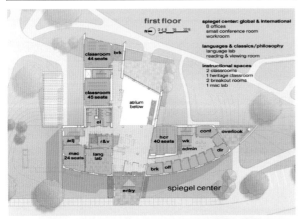

first floor

N ⊙ 0 4 8   16   32ft

spiegel center: global & international
8 offices
small conference room
workroom

languages & classics/philosophy
language lab
reading & viewing room

instructional spaces
2 classrooms
1 heritage classroom
2 breakout rooms
1 mac lab

spiegel center

ground floor

N ⊙ 0 4 8   16   32ft

multipurpose & support space
atrium
atrium storage
recycling/loading
mechanical/electrical

instructional spaces
1 classroom
3 mac labs
1 breakout room

multimedia studio
production studio
control room
equipment storage
green-screen room
2 editing rooms

Figure 4.14
Schematic floor plans clearly evolved from the earlier studies
shown in Figure 4.13 (courtesy of Goody Clancy).

water-conserving toilets. Although the client was
uncertain whether to pursue LEED certification, they
supported the desire for a sustainable building to the
maximum extent possible within the budget.

Other critical factors shaping the design
This is a very visible site and the client was quite
firm that no mechanical / electrical / plumbing
equipment should be visible from the quad.
This directly influenced where air-handling
equipment, the chiller, boiler flue, and other
items could and could not be located.

Code issues, sun control, and cost influenced the
atrium configuration. Initially, the atrium concept was
to link all four levels of the building. However, after
further study and analysis of the cost as well as code
issues including smoke control, atrium exhaust
(large fans), and air intake, it was reduced by one floor.
The top floor, primarily smaller spaces such as offices,
no longer participates in the atrium volume and views,
which actually makes that space a bit quieter and more
private. The three-storey glass walls face east and
south, so sun control was an important issue.
In addition to using low-E glass to reduce heat gain,
the architects incorporated zones of frit for sun control.
Nevertheless, they felt this kind of space could be
allowed to be brighter than the classrooms and other
functionally driven spaces in the building's wings.

RWU's Global Heritage theme is meant to express the
university's commitment to understanding its place
in the largest possible context, and to celebrate many
diverse cultures. The university's extensive language

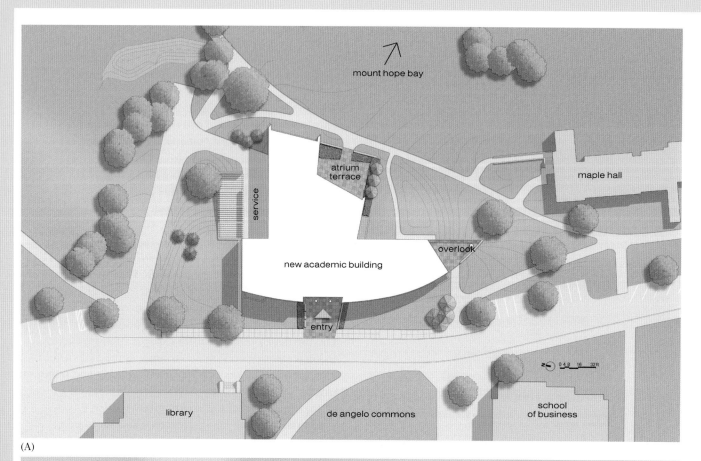

mount hope bay

atrium terrace

service

maple hall

overlook

new academic building

entry

0 4 8   16   32 ft

library

de angelo commons

school of business

(A)

(B)

(C)

Figure 4.15
(A) Schematic site plan showing the new building and its immediate
context (courtesy of Goody Clancy). (B) Building section through atrium.
Note that the lower level is on grade (on the left) as is the first floor on
the opposite side (on the right). (C) Rendering of the atrium (rendering
by Thomas Yamamoto, courtesy of Goody Clancy).

program and study abroad programs are housed in this building, along with the Spiegel Center for Global and International Programs.

The Global Heritage theme, "Learning to Bridge the World," is manifest in the atrium where the architects designed (together with their graphic design consultants) a multi-storey silk-screened graphic paneled wall that depicts the continents.
The continents are formed from graphic "heritage icons" that serve almost as pixels. There are 20 icons or medallions featured, with four each representing the cultures of Africa, Asia, the Americas, Europe, and the Middle East. Each icon is drawn from the respective culture's imagery. The icons correspond to the cultures represented in the heritage classrooms. (See Figure 4.15B.)

There are six Heritage classrooms, each of which is outfitted uniquely, including commissioned arts and crafts pieces, display cases for artifacts, and historic images as full-height wall panels. These cultures were selected because they each have a relationship to the local context (Bristol, African-American, Italian, Portuguese, Native American, and Latino).

Cost issues
The scope of work—size of the building—was reduced after schematic design due to high cost estimates in an escalating construction market. The atrium was reduced in volume; the footprint of the building was reduced; a Heritage classroom was pushed into the smaller footprint; the newsroom, a conference room, and a lounge were eliminated. However, the completed project stayed within the approved budget, including change orders.

The global market for curtainwall led to cost and delivery concerns, and issuance of an early steel bid package. At the time, steel pricing was low, so the construction manager recommended buying it early to lock in the cost. Curtainwall was typically also a long-lead item due to the global demand, so the construction manager suggested it be another early bid package to make sure the curtainwall could be procured within the timeframe. However, the design team decided not to do this, as it would have accelerated the design too dramatically, potentially leading to cost premiums. The curtainwall ended up arriving in plenty of time so did not delay the schedule.

Figure 4.16 (A) (Below)
Quad-side elevation studies. (A) Early scheme that was rejected. (rendering by Thomas Yamamoto, courtesy of Goody Clancy).

(B)

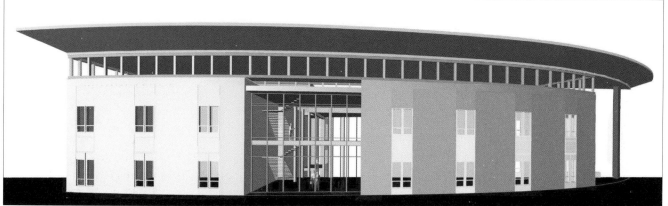

(C)

(D)

Figure 4.16 (B, C and D)

(B) The power of the curve is evident in this perspective. Note how materials are composed with brick at each end and cast stone in the middle (rendering by Thomas Yamamoto, courtesy of Goody Clancy). (C) The entry reveals views to the atrium and beyond; the roof appears to float above a band of windows on the upper floor. (D) The materials composition changes, with brick extending to frame the recessed entry (courtesy of Goody Clancy).

Figure 4.17
The quad-side elevation as built (© Anton Grassl/Esto).

Materials

On the exterior, brick and cast stone on the quad side relate to the neighboring buildings and "ground" the building in its campus context. In contrast, glass and curtainwall systems, metal (rainscreen) wall panels, metal column enclosures, and stainless steel cable railings relate to the waterside in a more reflective, shimmering fashion (see elevations, Figures 4.16, 4.17, 4.18, and 4.19).

On the interior, wood paneling and trim in classrooms carry forward the campus tradition of warm, solid, and durable materials in instructional spaces. Porcelain tile, metal wall panels, perforated metal ceiling systems, metal column enclosures, structural glass railings, and of course large expanses of glass in the atrium promote the transition from traditional campus to modern waterfront.

Building systems

Mechanical rooms were discreetly located at the ground floor and mechanical/roof level to be concealed from view as much as possible, as mandated by the client. The HVAC equipment included rooftop cooling towers, rooftop atrium exhaust fans, air handlers located in basement mechanical rooms, hot water boilers, water chiller, runtal radiators, finned tube radiation, radiant heat panels, fan coil units, and supplemental cooling units at computer rooms.

Energy-saving features include occupancy sensors to control the lighting and high-efficiency, low-flow, hands-free, sensor-controlled toilet fixtures.

State-of-the-art AV and IT systems included wireless network and internet access throughout the building, video conferencing capabilities, projection screens, and LCD screens. The multimedia classroom on the ground floor is the instructional technology showpiece of the building, serving not only as a specialized classroom, but also as a television studio simulator for students studying communications.

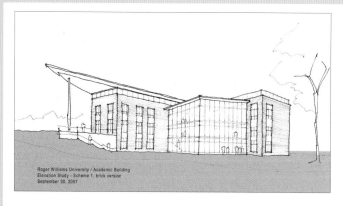

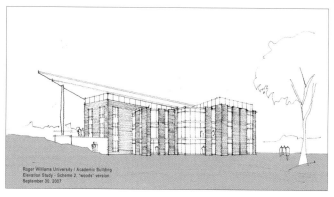

(A)

Figure 4.18

Bay-side elevation studies. (A) Brick "bookends" contrast with
glass atrium. (B) Brick alternates with glass to emphasize the
vertical dimension. (C and D) Brick evolves into metal panels with
continuous horizontal metal bands linking the distinct masses
(rendering (D) by Thomas Yamamoto, courtesy of Goody Clancy).

(C)

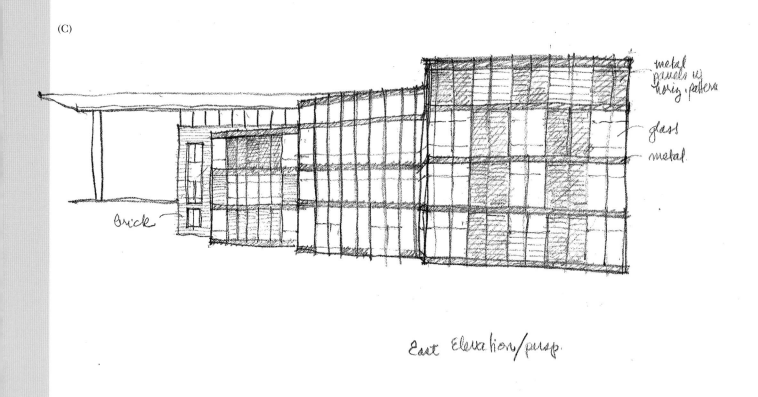

(D)

Figure 4.19
The bay-side elevation as built. Note metal-clad "fin walls" express the
radiating geometry (© Anton Grassl/Esto).

Autodesk A/E/C Division Headquarters

Architect and Engineer: *KlingStubbins; Scott Simpson, FAIA, LEED AP. Senior Director; Chris Leary, AIA, LEED AP, Project Manager; Sarah Springer, IIDA, LEED AP, Designer.* Construction Manager: *Tocci Building Companies.*

What better idea than to use the client's own software tools to generate the design for their new headquarters in order to demonstrate how to advance the design process? Autodesk is a company that has developed Building Information Modeling (BIM) software in addition to the well-known AutoCad and other applications. The tools themselves, of course, did not determine the design, but in the hands of the skilled architects an intriguing design was produced that would not have been possible using conventional means. A distinctive modular ceiling design arose from both practical and symbolic aspects that have significance for the client and striking visual impact for building users and visitors.

This project is particularly instructive in showing how a meaningful design concept was derived from the client's wish to promote their product through a tangible result of its use. Moreover, the client's request for proposals contained three requirements that could be considered paradigm shifts in conducting architectural practice today: Integrated project delivery (IPD) using BIM, with a LEED Platinum rating. It is significant that when these project delivery strategies were applied to this project, a seemingly conventional fit-up of an existing suburban office building became something special.

The metrics for design success were clear and simple: (1) The job had to come in, on, or under budget; (2) the job had to comply with an extremely aggressive schedule; (3) the job had to demonstrate superior design quality; and (4) the job had to achieve a LEED Platinum rating. All four criteria were included as part of the request for proposals (RFP), and all four were met.

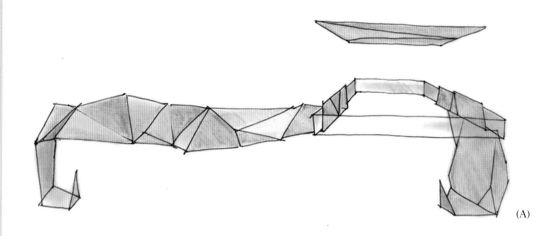

(A)

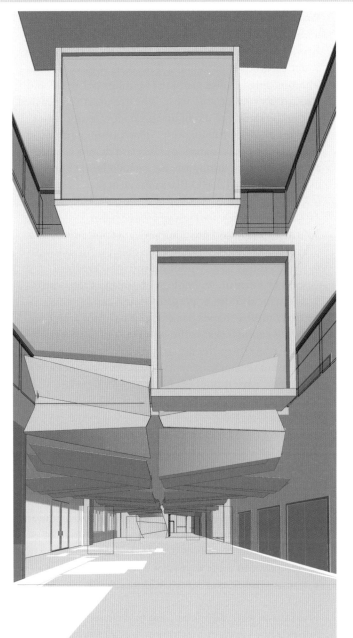

(B)

Figure 4.20
An early design study involved folded planes as depicted in (A) cross-sectional sketch from the Customer Briefing Center (CBC) on the left to the atrium on the right; (B) view of the CBC from the atrium; and (C) the atrium itself (© KlingStubbins).

(C)

Program summary

The project is a regional headquarters for Autodesk A/E/C Division, a major software company. The program included a 60,000 square-foot office fit-up that was to be the first-ever 100 percent IPD, 100 percent BIM, and LEED Platinum project in the United States. The program included the usual mix of offices and support areas as well as a "Halo" telepresence room, a cafeteria, and a "Customer Briefing Center" to highlight the client's products and services, in addition to a sophisticated IT system (a "regression farm" for testing software products).

Client preferences

The client, who operates millions of square feet of office space around the world, had predetermined corporate-wide standards with regard to program, office components, and finishes, all of which were included in the RFP.

The client wanted an atmosphere in which "quants" (the software engineers) could happily coexist with marketers. This was an architectural challenge because it required the integration of two entirely different subcultures in one open office. The quants, highly specialized technical staff, desired visual and acoustical privacy; they essentially work on demanding applied mathematics problems all day long. In their work, noise and casual social interaction can be especially distracting. By contrast, marketers are, by nature, much more social and thrive on collaboration and teamwork. Corporate leadership felt the need to be responsive to both groups of employees, but also needed to strike a balance in the design scheme. Their decision was to go with mostly open offices, with a minimum of closed-off spaces. Private offices would have full walls of glass. Low translucent panels for visual privacy between the desks (while sitting) and acoustical baffling in the open ceiling (to dampen noise) together serve to gracefully optimize both openness and privacy. Moreover, break rooms were placed around corners rather than in a direct line of sight from desk areas, so that they were accessible but not in the way (see Figure 4.24C).

Site and context influences

The site is in a suburban location, immediately adjacent to a major highway with direct on-ramp access, about 15 miles from Boston. There are highway views (the building is quite visible at 60 miles per hour) and also woods views to the west. The architects conducted careful modeling of daylighting, shadow studies, and sightlines on the BIM system. The vast majority of work stations have exterior views and do not require artificial lighting during the day, which helped greatly in achieving the LEED Platinum rating.

Architectural concept and organizational ideas

The architects used the company's software tools as a trigger to develop a bold design concept: An innovative modular ceiling as a symbol for the mathematical aspects of software technology. The notion of simple mathematical codes or patterns being combined to create complex shapes became the basis for a unique "flowing ceiling" that is the main design signature of the space. Early in the design process, Sarah Springer, the interior design principal, hit on the "boomerang" shape, and gave it double curvature so that when assembled and hung, there would be deliberate gaps that would enable projectors embedded in the ceiling to work on the vertical wall surfaces of the Customer Briefing Center. The curvature of the boomerangs was such that they could climb like ivy from floor to walls to ceiling, right up through the atrium. Taking it a step further, the BIM model of the ceiling design was transferred to CNC machines so that automatic routers could cut the boomerangs. The ceiling design is an excellent example of how design thinking, linked with technology, can achieve results that would otherwise not be possible (see Figures 4.21 and 4.22).

The offices were designed to maximize natural daylight and exterior views. A new three-storey atrium was punched in the existing building to provide vertical integration. The atrium is punctuated by projecting conference rooms that make for a visually exciting space, which helps tie all three floors of the office together (see Figure 4.23).

Figure 4.21
(A) The distinctive modular ceiling is the main design signature of the space. This schematic perspective view of the atrium and CBC is from the lobby. (B) A new three-storey atrium was carved out of the existing building as shown in this section (overleaf). Note how the ceiling "boomerangs" climb like ivy from floor to walls to ceiling, right up through the atrium (© KlingStubbins).

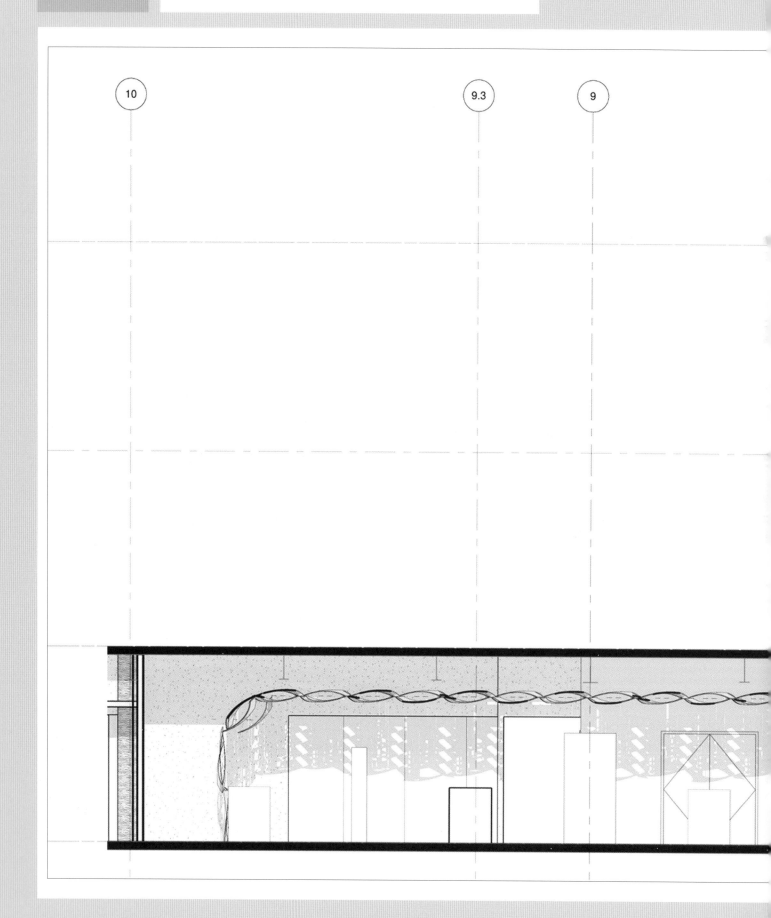

(A)

Figure 4.22
Modular ceiling details. (A) Built condition (© Jeff Goldberg/Esto).
(B) Ceiling pattern. (C) Group of six boomerangs. (D) Connection
detail (© KlingStubbins).

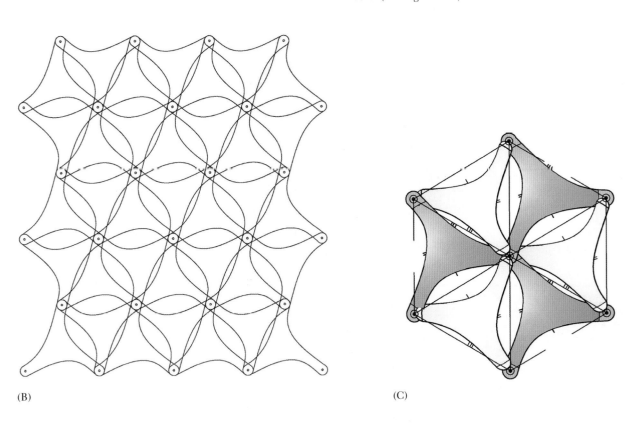

(B)

(C)

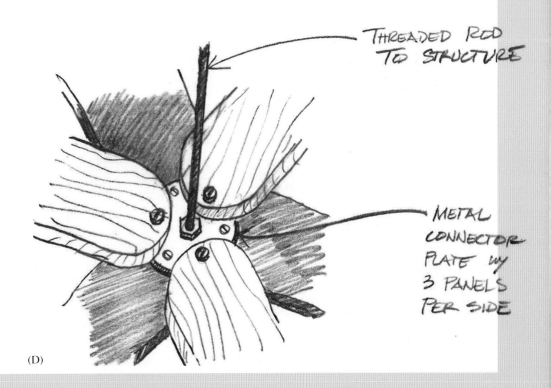

THREADED ROD
TO STRUCTURE

METAL
CONNECTOR
PLATE w/
3 PANELS
PER SIDE

(D)

(A)

Figure 4.23
(A and B) The new atrium ties
all three floors together and
is punctuated by projecting
conference rooms that animate the
space (© Jeff Goldberg/Esto).

(B)

Designer's agenda

As the design principal for the project, Sarah Springer concentrated on finding ways to express the client's unique corporate culture and work processes into the design concept. She felt that the new offices should reflect what the company did, and how they did it, and that the space should reinforce the overall sense of teamwork and collaboration that Autodesk was trying to promote. After all, staff literally spend more time in the office than they do with their families, and so Sarah wanted this place to feel like home.

Other critical factors shaping the design

Critical factors shaping the design included the constraints of existing conditions: This was a typical ordinary suburban office building shell that needed to be extraordinary on the inside. Working with the client's strict design standards but still achieving something special was a challenge. And speed was a major objective—the entire project was designed, documented, and delivered in only eight months. This required a lot of overlap between the designers and the construction management firm, Tocci. In the early stages, all key team members co-located at the KlingStubbins office, and then migrated to the Tocci office. Co-location included not only the architects and CM, but also engineers and major subcontractors to facilitate the collaborative process. A full IPD approach was a client requirement, so this led to unconventional contracts and risk management.

Cost issues

The client established a firm budget as a condition of the RFP, which could not be exceeded except for client-approved additions to the scope of work.

At several points during the project, the client decided to add scope (the atrium and cafeteria were two examples). Using BIM technology, the design team managed to model several possible alternates, price them with the assistance of the CM, and include them in the project without sacrificing time. In fact, during the course of the work, about 30 percent more scope was added, but the delivery date did not change.

The contract included both "no-sue" and "no change order" clauses, so that any cost overruns not involving scope expansion were automatically the responsibility of the IPD team.

By laser-scanning existing conditions at the very beginning of the job, the design team had exact measurements, which helped to avoid coordination errors in the field. Off-site prefabrication of ductwork, sprinkler piping, the ceiling system, and other components helped to both control cost and maintain the aggressive schedule.

Materials

Materials included drywall, floor-to-ceiling glass partitions, carpeting, and modular furniture. Bright accent colors were used to animate certain spaces, such as the break areas (see Figure 4.24C). Special feature: Innovative modular ceiling panels ("boomerangs") that flow through the space, curving up from the floor and through the atrium. These are double-curvature panels made of eucalyptus, manufactured on computer-driven CNC machines, run off of the BIM model. (Because of its fast growth rate, eucalyptus groves replenish themselves more rapidly than other sources of hardwood.)

Building systems

Steel frame, articulated pre-cast exterior, open ceilings, standard mechanical/electrical/plumbing (MEP) and sprinklers but with sophisticated building system controls, and innovative lighting arranged according to computer-modeled daylight studies comprise the major systems. Careful attention was paid to selecting MEP systems to reduce energy consumption and long-term maintenance costs, consistent with the client's mandate and the architect's vision.

Figure 4.24
(A) The double-curved panels flow from floor to ceiling of the CBC. (B) The panels have propagated to the third floor, and are visible through the glass railing. (C) (overleaf) Break areas, highlighted with accent colors, were placed around corners so they are accessible but not distracting from work stations (© Jeff Goldberg/Esto).

(A)

(B)

Index